Uncle Tom's Cabin
Indictment of Slavery

Titles in the
Words That Changed History series include:

The Declaration of Independence

The Emancipation Proclamation

The Nuremberg Laws

The Origin of Species

The U.S. Constitution

The King James Bible

The Liberator

Words
THAT
CHANGED
HISTORY

Uncle Tom's Cabin

Indictment of Slavery

by James Tackach

Lucent Books
P.O. Box 289011, San Diego, CA 92198-9011

On Cover: A lithograph engraved by Claude Regnier (1840-1896) from the book Uncle Tom's Cabin by Harriet Beecher Stowe (1811-1896).

Library of Congress Cataloging-in-Publication Data

Tackach, James.
    Uncle Tom's Cabin : indictment of slavery / James Tackach.
        p.   cm. — (Words that changed history)
    Includes bibliographical references and index.
    Summary: Discusses the circumstances that existed at the time Stowe wrote
her famous novel, the details of the book, and its impact on feelings about the
existence of slavery in the United States in the mid-nineteenth century.
    ISBN 1-56006-591-5 (lib. : alk. paper)
    1. Stowe, Harriet Beecher, 1811-1896. Uncle Tom's Cabin—Juvenile
liturature. 2. Liturature and society—United States—History—19th
century—Juvenile liturature. 3. Didactic fiction, America—History and
criticism—Juvenile liturature. 4. Southern States—In Liturature—Juvenile
liturature. 5. Plantation life in liturature—Juvenile liturature. 6. Afro-
Americans in liturature—Juvenile liturature. 7. Slavery in liturature—
Juvenile liturature. [1.Stowe, Harriet Beecher, 1811-1896. Uncle Tom's
Cabin. 2. American liturature—History and Criticism. 3. Slavery.] I. Title.
II. Series.

PS2954.U6 T34 2000
813'.3—dc21   99-051861

Contents

Foreword

"We hold these truths to be self-evident, that all men are created equal, that they are endowed by their Creator with certain unalienable Rights, that among these are Life, Liberty and the pursuit of Happiness." So states one of America's most cherished documents, the Declaration of Independence. These words ripple through time. They represent the thoughts of the Declaration's author, Thomas Jefferson, but at the same time they reflect the attitudes of a nation in which individual rights were trampled by a foreign government. To many of Jefferson's contemporaries, these words characterized a revolutionary philosophy of liberty. Many Americans today still believe the ideas expressed in the Declaration were uniquely American. And while it is true that this document was a product of American ideals and values, its ideas did not spring from an intellectual vacuum. The Enlightenment which had pervaded France and England for years had proffered ideas of individual rights, and Enlightenment scholars drew their notions from historical antecedents tracing back to ancient Greece.

In essence, the Declaration was part of an ongoing historical dialogue concerning the conflict between individual rights and government powers. There is no doubt, however, that it made a palpable impact on its times. For colonists, the Declaration listed their grievances and set out the ideas for which they would stand and fight. These words changed history for Americans. But the Declaration also changed history for other nations; in France, revolutionaries would emulate concepts of self-rule to bring down their own monarchy and draft their own philosophies in a document known as the Declaration of the Rights of Man and of the Citizen. And the historical dialogue continues today in many third world nations.

Lucent Books's Words That Changed History series looks at oral and written documents in light of their historical context and their lasting impact. Some documents, such as the Declaration, spurred people to immediately change society; other documents fostered lasting intellectual debate. For example, Charles Darwin's treatise *On the Origin of Species* did not simply extend the discussion of human origins, it offered a theory of evolution which eventually would cause a schism between some religious and scientific thinkers. The debate still rages as people on both sides reaffirm their intellectual positions, even as new scientific evidence continues to impact the issue.

Students researching famous documents, the time periods in which they were prominent, or the issues they raise will find the books in this series both compelling and useful. Readers will see the chain of events that give rise to historical events. They will understand through the examination of specific documents that ideas or philosophies always have their antecedents, and they will learn how these documents carried on the legacy of influence by affecting people in other places or other times. The format for the series emphasizes these points by devoting chapters to the political or intellectual climate of the times, the values and prejudices of the drafters or speakers, the contents of the document and its impact on its contemporaries, and the manner in which perceptions of the document have changed through time.

In addition to their format, the books in Lucent's Words That Changed History series contain features that enhance understanding. Many primary and secondary source quotes give readers insight into the thoughts of the document's contemporaries as well as those who interpret the document's significance in hindsight. Sidebars interspersed throughout the text offer greater examination of relevant personages or significant events to provide readers with a broader historical context. Footnotes allow readers to verify the credibility of source material. Two bibliographies give students the opportunity to expand their research. And an appendix that includes excerpts as well as full text of original documents gives students access to the larger historical picture into which these documents fit.

History is often shaped by words. Oral and written documents concretize the thoughts of a select few, but they often transform the beliefs of an entire era or nation. As Confucius asserted, "Without knowing the force of words, it is impossible to know men." And understanding the power of words reveals a new way of understanding history.

The Book That Started a Great War

Written documents sometimes change the course of history. For example, on October 31, 1517, a German priest named Martin Luther posted ninety-five theses declaring his religious principles on the door of a church in Wittenberg and ignited a religious reformation that profoundly altered the shape of European Christianity. On July 4, 1776, a group of American colonists signed the Declaration of Independence, which not only proclaimed the American colonies free from Great Britain, their mother country, but also articulated a slate of human rights that much of the civilized world has come to embrace.

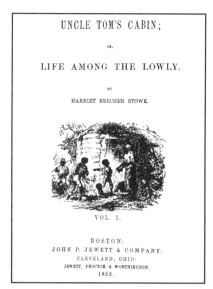

UNCLE TOM'S CABIN;

OR,

LIFE AMONG THE LOWLY.

BY

HARRIET BEECHER STOWE.

VOL. I.

BOSTON:
JOHN P. JEWETT & COMPANY.
CLEVELAND, OHIO:
JEWETT, PROCTOR & WORTHINGTON.
1852.

The title page from Harriet Beecher Stowe's influential novel.

On January 1, 1863, President Abraham Lincoln issued the Emancipation Proclamation, which virtually ended almost 250 years of American slavery.

Rarely, however, does a work of fiction have such a forceful impact on the course of history. Most people read novels for entertainment—to enjoy a good story. A particularly powerful novel might affect the thinking of individual readers and perhaps even prompt some to change their lives or attitudes in significant ways, but not often does a fictional story provoke an entire nation to change its policies. Political manifestos, constitutions, and court orders induce historical change; novels delight, enthrall, and amuse their readers.

Harriet Beecher Stowe's *Uncle Tom's Cabin* stands out as an exception to this general rule. No American novel has had a more immediate impact on its audience. Stowe's novel, published first serially in a weekly newspaper from 1851 to 1852 and soon thereafter in book format, moved an entire nation; it shaped public opinion and prompted citizens to action. It became the subject of political oratory, of fiery sermons delivered from the pulpits of American churches, and of scores of essays and articles in the daily press. Ultimately, Stowe's novel moved armies into battle; and when the fighting stopped, more than six hundred thousand Americans lay dead, and their nation was immensely changed.

The subject of Stowe's novel was American slavery, an institution that infected American soil in 1619 and remained stubbornly in place, at least in the Southern states, until 1865. The American Declaration of Independence of 1776 boldly announced that all citizens were entitled to "life, liberty, and the pursuit of happiness," but the framers of that document did not see it fit to eliminate slavery from their newborn nation. Ironically, the primary author of that declaration, Thomas Jefferson, owned a Virginia plantation maintained by more than two hundred slaves. By 1800, however, slavery had disappeared in the Northern United States, mainly because it had become unprofitable. The North's growing season was short, and Northern farmers could not feed, house, and clothe slaves for a whole year only to put them to work productively for three or four months.

In the South, however, slavery remained enormously profitable. After the turn of the nineteenth century, the North began to shift from an agricultural economy to a manufacturing and industrial

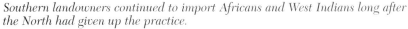

Southern landowners continued to import Africans and West Indians long after the North had given up the practice.

economy. The South remained agrarian, and slaves could play a vital role in an agricultural economy. With little training, they could learn to plow fields, sow seeds and harvest crops, care for animals, and perform other routine daily duties on a small farm or large plantation. By the middle of the nineteenth century, approximately 4 million African Americans worked as slaves on the farms and plantations of the South; its economy depended heavily on slave labor.

Uncle Tom's Cabin attacked American slavery on moral grounds. Stowe had been reared in an abolitionist family; her father, Lyman Beecher, a minister, was actively involved in the crusade to rid America of slavery, and he passed his values on to his children. At an early age,

Harriet Beecher had been taught that slavery was a grievous sin. The institution of slavery bonded human beings to masters to work for little or no pay; it allowed for slaves to be beaten severely for minor infractions; it resulted in the division of slave families when slave parents were sold to one master and the children to another. Stowe's powerful saga of a Kentucky slave named Uncle Tom exposed slavery's many misdeeds. Her novel jolted its readers, prompting abolitionists to double their efforts to eliminate slavery from the United States and awakening complacent Americans to the evils of an institution that they had essentially ignored or had judged to be benign.

Harriet Beecher Stowe's Uncle Tom's Cabin *reached deep into the American conscience, becoming a catalyst for the eventual end to slavery.*

Stowe's protest novel was by no means the first document to attack slavery; American abolitionist literature can be traced back to a manifesto by Samuel Sewall titled *The Selling of Joseph*, published in 1700. Nor did Stowe's book on its own abolish American slavery; it took Lincoln's Emancipation Proclamation, the North's victory in a bloody civil war, and an amendment to the U.S. Constitution to finally end slavery on American soil. But *Uncle Tom's Cabin* aroused the nation. It swelled the abolitionist ranks and pressured slaveholders to defend their institution more strenuously; it helped turn the United States into, in Lincoln's words, a "house divided against itself."[1]

Lincoln himself acknowledged the role that Stowe's novel had played in igniting the great civil war that ended American slavery when he met Stowe at a reception at the White House in 1862. "So you're the little woman who wrote the book that started this great war!"[2] the president reportedly exclaimed as he greeted the author of *Uncle Tom's Cabin*. Even the powerful president recognized the impact of Stowe's forceful novel.

CHAPTER 1 Slavery in America: 1619–1850

Slavery took root on the continent of North America in 1619, when a group of about twenty black Africans seized in their native continent were brought to the British colony in Jamestown, Virginia, and sold to settlers to labor on their farms. These were the first of a steady stream of Africans brought to America against their will and sold into slavery during the seventeenth century. During the eighteenth century, slave importation increased. Africans kidnapped on their own continent were traded in colonial seaport cities for sugar, molasses, rum, tobacco, and other American products, then sold at auctions to colonial farmers in search of cheap labor. This brisk slave trade that developed during the 1700s resulted in the importation of more than a half million Africans to toil in America as slaves. Slaves were also imported from the West Indies. The importation of slaves into America would become illegal in 1808, but the American-born descendants of the African and West Indian slaves remained in bondage

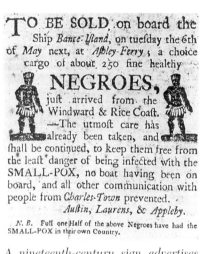

A nineteenth-century sign advertises smallpox-free slaves for sale.

for life, unless they were set free by their masters. By 1851, when Harriet Beecher Stowe conceived her antislavery novel, *Uncle Tom's Cabin*, approximately 4 million African Americans were held in bondage.

Slavery in Colonial America

Initially, slavery was not solely a Southern institution. By the middle of the eighteenth century, slavery existed in all thirteen of Great Britain's American colonies. In the Northern colonies, however, slavery was much less profitable than it was in the Southern colonies. The growing season in the Middle Atlantic and New England colonies was short, lasting from mid-May through September.

A Northern slave owner would have to support his slaves for the entire year, but they could be put to work effectively only during the spring and summer, when crops were planted, tended, and harvested. During the autumn and winter months, Northern slaves had little to do. In the South, however, the growing season was much longer, due to the South's milder climate. It became cost effective for Southern growers to maintain slaves to work on their farms and plantations. Hence, the economies of the Southern colonies remained essentially agricultural. The South's chief exports for trade were agricultural products—rice, tobacco, indigo, and later cotton. Because these crops were planted, tended, and harvested mainly by Southern slaves, the Southern colonies became increasingly dependent on slave labor.

By the time of the American Revolution, slavery was already beginning to disappear in Great Britain's Northern colonies. By the early 1770s, a few of the colonies had enacted emancipation statutes—laws that immediately freed all slaves or gradually eliminated slavery over a

Indentured Servitude

Parallel to the development of slavery in America was the development of a system of indentured servitude. Indentured servants were most likely white Englishmen and -women who desired to leave their native country and take advantage of cheap land and opportunities in America, but who lacked the finances to pay for overseas passage and set up homes in the New World. So these individuals contracted themselves to an American farmer or craftsman to work for a period of years in exchange for passage to America, food, clothing, housing, and sometimes a small salary. At the end of the indentureship, which usually lasted from four to ten years, the indentured servant was free from his or her contract and was able to seek work, purchase land, or engage in a trade.

During the colonial era, about 250,000 indentured servants immigrated to America from Great Britain, and they played an important role in the American economy. Most worked as field hands on colonial farms and plantations. Others were taught trades such as blacksmithing, shipbuilding, and leather working. Many girls and women served as indentured domestic servants in colonial households.

Unlike slaves, indentured servants came to America willingly and were free men and women after their indentureship was complete.

Southern plantation owners supervise their slaves as they harvest rice on the Savannah River in Georgia.

period of time. For example, in 1774 the General Assembly of the Rhode Island colony banned the importation of slaves into the colony. Rhode Island lawmakers later decreed that the offspring of slaves would be considered free citizens, thereby guaranteeing that slavery would end in Rhode Island when existing slaves passed on.

The American Revolution

During the early 1770s, the relationship between the American colonies and Great Britain began to deteriorate. Disputes over taxation and colonial governance increased tensions between the colonies and their mother country, leading to civil unrest in some American cities. In Boston on March 5, 1770, a group of citizens began throwing snowballs at a company of British soldiers. The troopers returned the snowball fire with shots from their muskets, which resulted in the deaths of five colonials. The incident, which became known as the Boston Massacre, further damaged the relationship between the American colonies and England. Three years later, Boston colonials protesting a new tax on tea boarded British ships and dumped more than three hundred chests of tea into Boston Harbor. Great Britain responded by closing Boston Harbor to all trading vessels and disbanding some colonial legislative bodies.

In September 1774 colonial representatives met in Philadelphia as the First Continental Congress to discuss tactics for dealing with the crisis developing between the American colonies and Great Britain. At that meeting, the colonial representatives agreed to put the colonial militias on the alert to defend American civilians and their properties against any actions taken by British troops. Colonial militias began to collect and store weaponry to prepare for armed conflicts with British occupation forces.

In the spring of 1775, Massachusetts militiamen and British troops clashed at Lexington, Concord, and Bunker Hill. The other colonies rallied to the aid of Massachusetts. The Continental Congress commissioned George Washington, a Virginia plantation owner, or planter, and veteran of the French and Indian War, to command the colonial army in its battle with the British. The American Revolution had begun.

The Declaration of Independence

In June 1776 the Continental Congress met again in Philadelphia to discuss the developing conflict between the American colonies and Great Britain. By that time, the colonial representatives had given up any hope of a reconciliation between the colonies and their mother country. Both parties had already shed blood in the conflict; peacemakers from both sides could reach no common ground on which to base a treaty to end the conflict. In late June the Continental Congress

The incident, known as the Boston Massacre, resulted in the deaths of five colonials. British soldiers open fire on a group of snowball-wielding citizens.

assigned to Thomas Jefferson, a Virginia planter, the task of crafting a declaration of independence, a public document that would pronounce the colonials independent from Great Britain.

Jefferson and his colleagues were progressive thinkers who had in mind a new form of government for the American colonies, a philosophy of governing implemented nowhere in the world at that time. Their new nation would not be ruled by a king or monarch but by a government acting upon the will of the people and serving to protect the people's natural rights. "We hold these truths to be self-evident: That all men are created equal; that they are endowed by their Creator with certain inalienable rights; that among these are life, liberty, and the pursuit of happiness," wrote Jefferson; "that, to secure these rights, governments are instituted among men, deriving their just powers from the consent of the governed." Jefferson then asserted that governments destructive of these rights ought to be abolished and new governments formed.

Jefferson went on to list the ways in which King George III of Great Britain had abused the colonists' rights. He had dissolved the colonial legislative bodies, restricting the colonies' means of self-government. He had kept standing armies in the colonies during peace time. He had imposed harsh taxes on the colonies without their consent. He had deprived colonists of their right to a trial by jury. And he had "waged cruel war against human nature itself,

The rights of life, liberty, and the pursuit of happiness proclaimed by the framers of the Declaration of Independence did not apply to African slaves in America.

violating its most sacred right of life and liberty in the persons of a distant people who never offended him, captivating them into slavery in another hemisphere, or to incur miserable death in their transportation thither."[3]

But Jefferson's accusation concerning slavery never made the final draft of the declaration that was signed and delivered on July 4, 1776. The clauses on slavery were stricken from the document on the demand of Southern members of the Continental Congress, many of whom were the owners of large plantations highly dependent on slave labor. Hence, the inalienable rights of life, liberty, and the pursuit of happiness, deemed so important to the framers of the Declaration of Independence, would not apply to African American slaves.

The long war that followed the Declaration of Independence resulted in independence for the American colonies, but American slaves remained in bondage during and after that conflict. And the man who composed the colonies' Declaration of Independence, Thomas Jefferson, held slaves throughout his lifetime, fathered children by a slave woman, and kept those children in bondage.

The U.S. Constitution

The American Revolution ended in 1783. For several years, the American colonies functioned as a collection of loosely connected independent states. In 1787 representatives from each of England's former American colonies met in Philadelphia to discuss a plan to unite the independent states under a single form of government. After

When delegates drafted the Constitution at the Philadelphia Convention, slavery was not part of their discussions.

almost four months of vigorous debate, the delegates at the Philadelphia Convention formed the United States of America, a democratic republic held together by a constitution comprising seven articles and ten amendments referred to as the Bill of Rights.

Slavery was not a specific issue of discussion or debate at the Philadelphia Convention. No delegate proposed the abolition of slavery in the new American republic, though early in the convention George Mason, a representative from Virginia, alluded to the problem of slavery when he

17

asserted that "we ought to attend to the rights of every class of people" by providing "no less carefully" for the "happiness of the lowest than of the highest order of citizens."[4] But the delegates to the Philadelphia Convention were businessmen and landowners, men of property; they would ensure that their new government would protect the rights of property owners, including slaveholders.

The Machine That Made Slavery Profitable

In 1793 a New England inventor designed a machine that helped sustain slavery in the South. Eli Whitney, a Yale University graduate and the son of a Massachusetts farmer, invented a cotton gin, a machine that significantly reduced the processing of cotton. Before the arrival of Whitney's cotton gin, the tiny seeds had to be removed from a cotton ball by hand, a tedious and time-consuming process. The cotton gin, which essentially consisted of a box and two cylinders, efficiently separated the cotton from the seed. One cylinder, which contained wire teeth, separated the cotton fibers from the seed, and the second cylinder pulled the seed-free fiber from the wire teeth.

The cotton gin quickly made cotton the South's most profitable crop. There was a high demand for cotton in the textile mills of the North and in Great Britain as well. Since the cotton gin made the processing of cotton so much more efficient, Southern farmers rapidly expanded their cotton farms. The laborious task of planting, tending, and picking cotton in the hot and humid Southern summers fell to slaves. By the first decades of the nineteenth century, the South's economy had become highly dependent on cotton and on the slave labor that planted, picked, and processed it.

The cotton gin helped sustain the South's use of slaves by making cotton a profitable crop.

The new Constitution did not even mention the words *slave* or *slavery*. The document would include the Bill of Rights—a list of guarantees to American citizens, including freedom of religion, freedom of the press, freedom to assemble and protest without government interference, and the right to a fair trial. But the U.S. Constitution, which became the law of the land in 1791, allowed African Americans to be kept in bondage.

Compromises on Slavery

By 1804 slavery had been outlawed in the Northern states, but it remained legally in place throughout the South. Until 1820 the North and the South lived under an unstable compromise on the issue of slavery: Slavery would remain legal in the South but be prohibited in the North and would not be allowed to spread to any new territories acquired by the United States.

That arrangement became threatened in 1819, when the territory of Missouri applied for statehood. Congress had to debate whether Missouri would be added to the Union as a slave or free state. Adding Missouri as a slave state would break the unwritten contract between the North and the South that slavery would not be expanded to new states and territories. Moreover, in 1819 the United States comprised twenty-two states, eleven free states and eleven slave states. Adding another slave state to the Union would give the slave holding Southern states an advantage in the U.S. Senate, to which each state sent two delegates.

After a bitter debate, Congress found a compromise solution. Missouri would enter the Union as a slave state, and Maine would be admitted as a free state, an arrangement that would maintain the balance between free and slave states. Moreover, slavery would be outlawed in all U.S. territories north of latitude 36°30′.

The Missouri Compromise, also called the Compromise of 1820, diffused tensions between North and South for a time. The South seemed contented that slavery had been introduced to a new state, nullifying the old agreement that slavery would not be allowed to spread. The North seemed satisfied that a definite line, the 36°30′ latitude mark, had been drawn, north of which slavery could never be introduced.

But Thomas Jefferson, in retirement from politics at Monticello, his Virginia estate, and paying close attention to the debate over Missouri's statehood, worried that the latitude line of 36°30′ would someday become a barrier that would permanently divide his nation into antislavery and proslavery spheres. Jefferson sensed that this division might one day split the United States into two separate nations. In a letter to his friend John Holmes, Jefferson wrote, "A geographical line, coinciding with a marked

Jefferson and Slavery

The man who eloquently authored the Declaration of Independence was a Virginia aristocrat who owned slaves for all of his adult life. Although Jefferson often referred to slavery as a hideous evil, a foul blot on his country, and a contradiction of the principles on which American democracy was founded, his magnificent estate, Monticello, depended on the labor of scores of slaves for planting, caring for animals, and keeping the buildings and landscape in good repair.

In his famous work *Notes on the State of Virginia*, Jefferson outlined a plan to gradually end American slavery. He recommended freeing all slaves born in Virginia—after an emancipation plan was adopted—when those slaves reached a certain age, eighteen for females and twenty-one for males. The freed slaves would be transported to a colony outside the United States. If such a plan were enacted, slavery would disappear from Virginia in a generation. Despite working out this careful emancipation plan, Jefferson rarely freed his own slaves; most served on Jefferson's estate for their entire lives.

In 1998 genetic researchers found that the DNA of one of Jefferson's descendants matched the DNA of a descendent of Sally Hemmings, one of Jefferson's slaves who was a half sister of his wife,

Martha. Some historians had long speculated that Jefferson had had a sexual relationship with Hemmings after Martha's death and that children had resulted from that relationship, but no concrete proof existed to determine that Jefferson had slave offspring. The 1998 study made it virtually certain that Jefferson had children by Hemmings and that those children remained in slavery as long as Jefferson lived.

Thomas Jefferson

principle, moral and political, once conceived and held up to the angry passions of men, will never be obliterated; and every new irritation will mark it deeper and deeper."[5]

The Growth of the Abolitionist Movement

Although the Missouri Compromise seemed to ease tensions between the North and the South, Northerners opposed to slavery found the agreement distasteful because it had allowed slavery to be extended to a new state, opening the door for slavery's further expansion. Before 1820 the number of American abolitionists—citizens calling for an immediate end to slavery—was small, and abolitionists were often labeled radicals or fanatics. After 1820, however, the abolitionist movement gained momentum from a wave of other social reform movements—religious reform, educational reform, and a women's rights movement—that spread across the United States. The Mis-

William Lloyd Garrison warned that if slaves were not freed, they would eventually revolt against their masters.

souri Compromise further energized abolitionists; their movement gained supporters, and those supporters became more vocal.

In 1829 David Walker, the son of a slave who lived as a free man in Boston, inspired the abolitionist cause when he published and distributed a pamphlet titled *Walker's Appeal in Four Articles*. *Walker's Appeal*, written in an eloquent and fiery style, demanded an immediate end to slavery in the United States. Walker warned that the nation would face certain disaster unless it freed its people in bondage: "Perhaps they will laugh at or make light of this, but I tell you Americans! that unless you speedily alter your course, *you* and your Country are gone!!!!! For God Almighty will tear up the face of the earth!!!"[6] Walker died shortly after his *Appeal* was published, but the influential document was reprinted and widely distributed during the next thirty years.

On January 1, 1831, William Lloyd Garrison, an abolitionist orator and writer from Massachusetts, added his eloquent voice to the

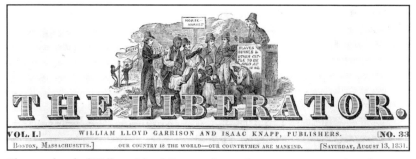

The masthead of William Lloyd Garrison's antislavery newspaper, the Liberator.

abolitionist cause. On that date, Garrison printed the first edition of an antislavery newspaper titled the *Liberator*. An editorial in that first edition boldly asserted Garrison's mission: "I shall strenuously contend for the immediate enfranchisement of our slave population . . . I am in earnest—I will not equivocate—I will not excuse—I will not retreat a single inch—AND I WILL BE HEARD."[7] That first issue of the *Liberator* also warned that if slavery were not immediately abolished in the United States, the slaves would eventually revolt against their masters and bathe the South in blood.

Nat Turner's Revolt

An event that occurred during the summer of 1831 suggested that Garrison's prediction was on the mark. That August, Nat Turner, a slave preacher bonded to a Virginia plantation, and a handful of followers launched a twelve-hour slave rebellion. Turner and his men acquired weapons, then moved from farm to farm killing the white masters and their families and liberating the slaves. During one night of terror, Turner and his band of rebels, whose number swelled to eighty escaped slaves, killed sixty white people, including children.

After his gruesome work was done, Turner fled into the Virginia countryside and remained at large for several weeks. He was finally captured and executed for his deeds that night. But his execution did little to alleviate the dread of slaveholders throughout the South, who feared that bloody rebellions like Turner's could be repeated throughout the South, leading to a widespread slave rebellion supported by thousands of runaway slaves hell-bent on exacting vengeance upon their masters. Before his death, Turner narrated his tale to a recorder, who published it as a pamphlet titled *The Confessions of Nat Turner*, another volume in the growing body of abolitionist writing being published in the United States.

Southerners blamed vocal abolitionists like Garrison for Turner's rebellion. Abolitionists were accused of inciting the slaves and urging them to take up arms against their owners. But Garrison was not a man to be intimidated. In 1833 he formed the American Anti-Slavery Society, an organization devoted to erasing slavery from the United States.

A Nation Divided

Proslavery Southerners struck back at Garrison and his abolitionist followers by disrupting his rallies, often with violence. Mailbags containing abolitionist literature were confiscated and burned by proslavery factions. In 1837 Elijah Lovejoy, an abolitionist editor living in Alton, Illinois, became the object of an attack by an angry mob of two hundred proslavery individuals. The mob surrounded the offices of Lovejoy's newspaper, the *Observer*, and demanded his surrender. Lovejoy or one of his workers fired a shot into the mob, killing a man. The crowd rushed Lovejoy's building. When he appeared at the door ready to defend himself, Lovejoy was shot to death.

News of Lovejoy's death spread quickly, shocking the nation. Americans were now killing Americans over the issue of slavery. As

Nat Turner was captured in Virginia and executed for the murders of over sixty white slave-owning families.

Jefferson had predicted, the nation seemed bitterly and irreparably torn apart over an institution that had been part of American life for more than two hundred years. But intimidation could not stop the abolitionist wave that was sweeping the North. Garrison and his supporters—Theodore Weld, Angelina and Sarah Grimké, and Wendell Phillips—doubled their efforts. In 1841 Frederick Douglass, a runaway Maryland slave, joined the abolitionist crusade. Douglass moved audiences with his riveting speeches based on his own firsthand knowledge of slavery's hardships. In 1845 Douglass, a self-taught reader and writer, published his autobiography *Narrative of the Life of an American Slave*, which quickly became a bestseller.

The Compromise of 1850

During the 1840s, tensions between the North and the South escalated, though both sides prudently avoided a deadly confrontation to provoke the crisis that would permanently rend the Union in two or lead to a civil war. During the late 1840s, however, another dispute arose between the North and the South that put the nation on the brink of civil war. The United States had acquired territory comprising New Mexico and California as a result of the Mexican War, waged from 1846 through 1848, and Congress began debating whether slavery should be legal in this new territory. The debate was predictably bitter. Many senators and congressmen from the North opposed any extension of slavery; meanwhile, the elected officials of the South opposed any restriction placed on slavery by the federal government. The matter was finally resolved when three distinguished senators— Henry Clay of Kentucky, Daniel Webster of Massachusetts, and Stephen Douglas of Illinois—brokered a resolution known as the Compromise of 1850.

The compromise had four major components. First, California was admitted to the United States as a free state. Second, Utah and New Mexico were established as U.S. territories, with the issue of slavery to be determined by a vote of the inhabitants of each territory. Third, the trading, buying, and selling of slaves in Washington, D.C., was outlawed. And fourth, a strict fugitive slave law was passed, enabling slave owners to recover runaway slaves more easily than before.

The Compromise of 1850 succeeded in delaying a civil war between the Northern and Southern states, but neither side was ultimately satisfied with the agreement. The South opposed the admission of a free state without the simultaneous admission of a slave state; now the Union would comprise sixteen free states and only fifteen slave states. Northern abolitionists, in turn, found the Fugitive Slave Law especially distasteful.

$200 Reward.

RANAWAY from the subscriber, on the night of Thursday, the 30th of Sepember,

FIVE NEGRO SLAVES,

To-wit : one Negro man, his wife, and three children.

The man is a black negro, full height, very erect, his face a little thin. He is about forty years of age, and calls himself *Washington Reed*, and is known by the name of Washington. He is probably well dressed, possibly takes with him an ivory headed cane, and is of good address. Several of his teeth are gone.

Mary, his wife, is about thirty years of age, a bright mulatto woman, and quite stout and strong.

The oldest of the children is a boy, of the name of FIELDING, twelve years of age, a dark mulatto, with heavy eyelids. He probably wore a new cloth cap.

MATILDA, the second child, is a girl, six years of age, rather a dark mulatto, but a bright and smart looking child.

MALCOLM, the youngest, is a boy, four years old, a lighter mulatto than the last, and about equally as bright. He probably also wore a cloth cap. If examined, he will be found to have a swelling at the navel.

Washington and Mary have lived at or near St. Louis, with the subscriber, for about 15 years.

It is supposed that they are making their way to Chicago, and that a white man accompanies them, that they will travel chiefly at night, and most probably in a covered wagon.

A reward of $150 will be paid for their apprehension, so that I can get them, if taken within one hundred miles of St. Louis, and $200 if taken beyond that, and secured so that I can get them, and other reasonable additional charges, if delivered to the subscriber, or to THOMAS ALLEN, Esq., at St. Louis, Mo. The above negroes, for the last few years, have been in possession of Thomas Allen, Esq., of St. Louis.

WM. RUSSELL.

ST. LOUIS, Oct. 1, 1847.

An 1847 advertisement offers a reward for the capture and return of five runaway slaves.

The Fugitive Slave Law called for the appointment of federal commissioners to seek and apprehend runaway slaves. These commissioners, who would be paid ten dollars for each runaway slave they returned to his or her owner, could force citizens in the North to form posses to capture the escapees. Moreover, citizens who assisted runaway slaves could be fined up to one thousand dollars and sent to prison for up to six months. African Americans identified as runaway slaves and captured could be returned to their alleged owners without the right of a jury trial.

Opposition to the Fugitive Slave Law

Northerners deeply objected to the stipulation in the law that compelled them to help arrest a runaway slave in a free state, where slavery was itself prohibited by law. Before the passage of the Fugitive Slave Law, slaves who had escaped from the South and reached the North safely were considered free; now, great efforts would be taken to return the runaways to their masters. Many abolitionists publicly denounced the Fugitive Slave Law and pledged to continue to abet runaway slaves who wished to flee to Canada, where the law did not apply. Abolitionists denounced

Senator Webster of Massachusetts for being one of the authors of this new law.

Shortly after the law was passed, a slave owner from Georgia sent two federal commissioners to apprehend William Craft, a slave who had escaped from Georgia and found safe haven in Boston two years earlier. Theodore Parker, a Boston minister and vocal abolitionist, hid Craft in his home, then sent the escaped slave to safety in England. After sending Craft abroad, Parker sent a searing letter to President Millard Filmore in Washington. "I would rather lie all my life in jail, and starve there, than refuse to protect one of these parishioners of mine," wrote Parker. "You cannot think that I am to stand by and see my own church carried off to slavery and do nothing."[8]

Abolitionist authors attacked the Fugitive Slave Law in essays, editorials, and speeches. Henry David Thoreau, the writer and philosopher from Concord, Massachusetts, published an essay titled "Slavery in Massachusetts," in which he asserted that the Fugitive Slave Law "rises not to the level of the head; its natural habitat is the dirt. It was born and bred, and has its life only in the dust and mire. . . . Trample it under foot."[9]

Outraged by the Fugitive Slave Law, Harriet Beecher Stowe began writing Uncle Tom's Cabin.

Other writers energized the abolitionist cause: the poets John Greenleaf Whittier and Henry Wadsworth Longfellow, the attorney and orator Wendell Phillips, and the women's rights activists Sarah and Angelina Grimké.

Some abolitionists maintained that writing against slavery was too tame a response; they vowed to murder federal commissioners who tried to capture runaway slaves living in the North. In Christiana, Pennsylvania, a Quaker community friendly to runaway slaves, a Maryland slave owner was shot to death when he came looking for two of his slaves who had escaped two years earlier.

Harriet Beecher Stowe Reacts

One author especially outraged by the Fugitive Slave Law was Harriet Beecher Stowe, a New Englander by birth, who, in 1850, was living in

Cincinnati, Ohio. Stowe was not a writer with a national reputation. In 1843 she had published a volume of short stories and sketches titled *The Mayflower*. Her family members, however, were active in the abolitionist cause. In 1837 Stowe's sister, Catharine Beecher, had published a volume titled *Essay on Slavery*. Her brother, Henry Ward Beecher, a nationally known clergyman living in New York, denounced slavery from the pulpit. Her husband, Calvin Stowe, was a theology professor engaged in the abolitionist crusade.

Late in 1850 Isabella Beecher, Harriet Beecher Stowe's sister-in-law who was living in Boston and was attuned to the debate about the Fugitive Slave Law, urged Harriet to lend her pen to the abolitionist battle. "Now, Hattie, if I could use a pen as you can, I would write something that would make this whole nation feel what an accursed thing slavery is,"[10] wrote Isabella in a letter to her sister-in-law. Shortly after receiving that letter, Harriet wrote to her husband, Calvin, who was traveling, and referred to her sister-in-law Isabella's advice: "I shall write that thing if I live."[11] That response was the genesis of *Uncle Tom's Cabin*, the novel that would invigorate abolitionists and prompt thousands of other Americans who had previously tolerated slavery to join the campaign to eradicate the institution from American soil. Stowe's book would also push the nation toward civil war.

CHAPTER 2

The Novelist and Her Great Novel

The author of *Uncle Tom's Cabin* was a New Englander by birth and a Midwesterner by migration. Harriet Beecher was born in Litchfield, Connecticut, on June 14, 1811. Her father, Lyman Beecher, was a Congregationalist minister; her mother, Roxana Foote Beecher, died when Harriet was only five years old, so Harriet was cared for by her older sister, Catharine, who would become a pioneer in the field of women's education. In 1823 Catharine established the Hartford Female Seminary, a postelementary school that provided a thorough liberal arts education for female students, who, until that time, learned only the domestic arts such as homemaking and child care. At age thirteen Harriet enrolled in her sister's school and accepted a teaching position there upon graduation.

Had Harriet Beecher remained in New England, she might never have written *Uncle Tom's Cabin*. In 1832, however, Reverend Beecher received an offer to become the president of Lane Theo-

Harriet (bottom right) came from a family that was deeply committed to the abolishment of slavery.

Dred: A Tale of the Great Dismal Swamp

In 1856 Harriet Beecher Stowe would publish a second antislavery novel titled *Dred: A Tale of the Great Dismal Swamp*. This novel did not receive the attention that *Uncle Tom's Cabin* received, nor did it enjoy the huge sales of the early novel. And literary historians and critics do not generally believe that *Dred* is as powerful a novel as *Uncle Tom's Cabin*.

In some ways, *Dred* presents a more radical attack on the institution of slavery. The main character, Dred, is the son of a historical figure hanged for igniting a slave rebellion in South Carolina. Unlike Uncle Tom, Dred escapes from slavery and hides in a swamp, planning a slave insurrection. He imagines himself as a contemporary Moses who will lead his people from the captivity of slavery to freedom. In *Uncle Tom's Cabin*, Stowe's protagonist, Uncle Tom, copes with slavery through prayer, patience, and the firm belief that his suffering on Earth is temporary while his reward in heaven will be eternal. In *Dred*, however, Stowe suggests that more activist strategies need to be taken by slaves to deal with their situation.

Stowe appended to *Dred* the text of *The Confessions of Nat Turner*, the autobiography of the man who began a slave revolt in Virginia in 1831 that resulted in the deaths of sixty white people.

logical Seminary in Cincinnati, Ohio, and the entire Beecher family moved to the Midwest. In Ohio, Harriet Beecher came into direct contact with slaves and slavery for the first time, and she began to gather the material for her famous antislavery novel.

Life in Cincinnati

In Cincinnati Catharine and Harriet established the Western Female Institute with Catharine as president and Harriet performing the dual role of chief assistant and faculty member. A year after moving to Cincinnati, Harriet published her first book, *Primary Geography for Children*. She also began writing short stories and sketches that would be collected several years later and published in a volume titled *The Mayflower; or Sketches of Scenes and Characters Among the Descendants of the Pilgrims*.

The Beecher household was one in which books were read and the ideas of the day, including the controversies surrounding slavery, were earnestly discussed. Reverend Beecher opposed slavery; he considered it a grievous sin and a moral outrage. Unlike many fathers of the mid–nineteenth century, Reverend Beecher did not try to shield his

Henry Ward Beecher

Harriet Beecher Stowe's younger brother, Henry Ward Beecher, became one of the most famous clergymen in American history. Henry was born in 1813, and he followed the career path of his father, Lyman, who, by the time of Henry's birth, was a nationally known Congregationalist minister, having founded the American Bible Society. After serving congregations in Indiana, Henry moved to the East. In 1847 he became the pastor of Plymouth Church in Brooklyn, New York. Henry used his pulpit as a forum from which to articulate his views on slavery, women's suffrage, and other political issues of the mid–nineteenth century. He became one of America's foremost critics of slavery; and he worked with mid–nineteenth century feminists in their efforts to gain American women the right to vote.

In 1875 Reverend Henry Beecher became the central figure in one of the nineteenth century's most noteworthy scandals. He was accused of having an adulterous affair with one of his parishioners, Mrs. Theodore Tilton. Reverend Beecher faced two trials for this alleged affair, a civil trial and a church trial, but he was ultimately

exonerated of all charges, though many believed that justice was not served by his acquittals. Nonetheless, Reverend Beecher avoided conviction and was able to remain in his influential position at Plymouth Church for the remainder of his career.

Henry Ward Beecher, a minister and younger brother to Harriet, used his pulpit to spread his antislavery message.

daughters from controversial political or social issues such as the national debate that was taking place over slavery. The Beecher sisters were encouraged to develop and articulate their own ideas and to write as well. In 1837 Catharine published a book titled *Essay on Slavery*, and the members of the Beecher family read and discussed an 1839 text edited by Theodore Weld, the abolitionist writer and orator, titled *American Slavery as It Is: Testimony of a Thousand Witnesses.*

Theodore Weld's abolitionist writings influenced the entire Beecher family.

After Harriet published her first book, she was invited to join the Semi-Colon Club, a Cincinnati literary society. During the club's meetings, members discussed books and the issues of the day; they also encouraged each other to write and share their work with the other members of the club. Catharine also joined the society, and the Beecher sisters became active members.

Marriage and Family

After joining the Semi-Colon Club, Harriet Beecher became close friends with two of its members, Calvin and Eliza Stowe. Calvin was the professor of biblical literature at Lane Theological Seminary. In 1834, Eliza died during an epidemic of cholera that swept through Cincinnati, and Harriet and Calvin became closer friends as a result of their shared grief. On January 6, 1836, Calvin and Harriet were married in a small and quiet ceremony at the Beecher home. They looked forward to starting a family.

Harriet Beecher Stowe gave birth to twin girls on September 29, 1836. Calvin insisted on naming the girls after his two wives, so they were given the names Eliza and Harriet. The younger Harriet became known in the Stowe family as "Hatty." During the next fourteen years, Harriet gave birth five times and suffered several miscarriages. Pregnancy and childbirth took a toll on Harriet, who was a small woman, barely five feet tall. For example, while carrying her fourth child, Frederick, who was born in 1840, Harriet endured a neurological disorder that impaired her eyesight. She also contracted cholera in 1845. In 1846, weakened from disease

Catharine Beecher

Harriet Beecher Stowe's older sister, Catharine Beecher, became a pioneer in American education, reforming educational curricula for female students.

Catharine's goal was not to become a famous educator. Born in 1800, she reached adulthood at a time when most American women had no career goals outside of the home. Catharine intended to marry and raise a family; she planned for a career as a mother and homemaker. When Catharine was twenty-two years old, however, her fiancé, Alexander Fisher, unexpectedly died, leaving Catharine to fend for herself as a single woman. Catharine found herself poorly equipped to compete in the mid–nineteenth-century American economy. She had attended Miss Pierce's Female Academy, a school for young women that stressed the domestic arts such as sewing, cooking, and child care. Young men of the time who entered the academies took courses in chemistry, mathematics, history, and other subjects that would prepare them for professional careers.

Catharine Beecher made it her goal to change women's education, to bring into the female academies the rigid liberal arts curriculum that would prepare young women for professional endeavors if they did not become mothers and homemakers. To achieve that goal, Catharine established the Hartford Female Seminary. She disliked teaching, so she performed the various administrative duties and hired others to teach, including men to teach in the natural sciences. Catharine also brought to Hartford Female Seminary guest lecturers such as Sarah and Angelina Grimké, two Quakers who were active in the abolitionist cause.

Catharine Beecher was politically conservative. For example, she believed that women should not strive to gain the right to vote or run for public office. But in the area of education, she became a revolutionary by completely reforming schooling for American women.

and miscarriages, Harriet traveled to Brattleboro, Vermont, and spent ten months in a rehabilitation center to regain her health and strength. While she was away, her sisters and relatives cared for her family.

Exposure to Slavery

Ohio bordered two slave states, Virginia and Kentucky. The city of Cincinnati is located on the Ohio River, the boundary separating

Ohio and Kentucky. The summer after moving to Ohio, Harriet and a friend traveled to Kentucky to visit acquaintances in that state. It was her first exposure to slavery. She witnessed slaves working hard in the fields on farms and plantations in Kentucky. Cincinnati was also an important riverport. Products were loaded on boats and barges in Cincinnati and sent downriver toward the Mississippi River, into which the Ohio River emptied. Products from the Southern states were sent up the Mississippi and Ohio Rivers for sale in Illinois and Ohio. Very often Southern boats were manned by slaves, and Harriet could see them performing the arduous task of loading and unloading goods when Southern ships ported in Cincinnati.

Before the passage of the Fugitive Slave Law of 1850, Kentucky slaves who could escape from bondage and cross the Ohio River could live as free men and free women in Ohio, which was a free state, or move on to Canada through the Underground Railroad—a series of houses in the North where runaway slaves could be safely hidden. Once Harriet's father and brother sheltered an escaped slave woman who had crossed the Ohio River into Cincinnati and took her

While touring the South, Harriet witnessed slaves hard at work. This experience influenced the content of Uncle Tom's Cabin.

in a wagon to an Underground Railroad station. During the 1840s, Harriet also taught the children of former slaves in her school.

Harriet's first-hand experiences with slaves and former slaves would harden her opposition to slavery and later serve as the material for *Uncle Tom's Cabin*. For example, Harriet would use the story of the fugitive slave woman helped by her father and brother as the basis for an episode in the novel during which a slave named Eliza crosses the Ohio River on ice floes and escapes into Ohio.

A Family Tragedy

During the mid–nineteenth century, the infant mortality rate was very high. Outbreaks of smallpox, typhoid fever, and other deadly diseases were frequent due to impure food and water and unsanitary living conditions. Because vaccinations, antibiotics, and other defenses against disease had not yet been developed, disease spread quickly, resulting in epidemics that took hundreds of lives. Children were, of course, particularly vulnerable to disease.

In the summer of 1849, a cholera epidemic swept through Cincinnati. Cholera is a bacterial infection whose source is often contaminated food or water. The infection attacks the intestines, causing high fever, vomiting, diarrhea, and severe loss of bodily fluids. Untreated, cholera can often be fatal, particularly when the disease is con-

Slave auctions often separated children from their parents. Harriet felt deeply connected to a slave mother's sense of loss after her son's death from cholera in 1849.

tracted by a young child. By late June, cholera was claiming the lives of one hundred people per day in and around Cincinnati.

In mid-July, eighteen-month-old Samuel Charles Stowe, Calvin and Harriet's sixth child, was stricken with cholera. For several days Harriet watched the baby suffer from the dreaded disease. She could do little for him but try to keep him comfortable and pray for his survival. But Samuel Charles died on July 26, after battling the disease for almost two weeks. Calvin was traveling overseas at the time of his son's death, and Harriet wrote to inform him of the terrible news: "I have just seen him in his death agony, looked at his imploring face when I could not help nor soothe nor do one thing, not one, to mitigate his cruel suffering, do nothing but pray in my anguish that he might die soon."[12] During that summer, more than nine thousand residents of Cincinnati and nearby towns died of cholera.

Harriet deeply mourned the death of young Samuel Charles. She had never felt such a loss before in her life. Dealing with her own grief, Harriet became acutely aware that slave women routinely experienced the loss of a child when that child was sold to another master. Harriet suddenly understood the pain of that kind of separation. She later wrote of Samuel Charles's death, "It was at *his* dying bed, and at *his* grave that I learnt what a poor slave mother may feel when her child is torn away from her."[13]

Moving East

Several months after Samuel Charles's death, Calvin received an offer to move back East to take a teaching position at Bowdoin College in Maine. Calvin accepted the job offer, and in the spring of 1850 Harriet, pregnant again, traveled to Maine with her three older children to set up household near Bowdoin College. She believed that the climate of Maine might be healthier than the climate of the Midwest, and she looked forward to leaving behind the terrible memories of Samuel Charles's death. Harriet left the younger children in Ohio with relatives and would not send for them until she had established a household in Maine.

On her way to Maine, Harriet and her children visited several relatives on the East Coast, including her brother and sister-in-law in Boston, Edward and Isabella Beecher. For several years Edward Beecher had been closely involved with Boston abolitionists, and he informed Harriet of his distaste for the proposed Fugitive Slave Law, which was being debated in Congress when Harriet and her children arrived. Like Edward, Harriet was outraged that such a law might be enacted, allowing runaway slaves to be apprehended in the North, and returned to the South, and punishing Northerners who assisted runaways.

Stowe encouraged her brother, Henry, to give voice to the abolitionist cause.

By the summer of 1850, Harriet had set up household in Brunswick, Maine. Calvin would begin his tenure at Bowdoin College that fall. In July, Harriet gave birth to her seventh child, Charles Edward.

Preparing to Write

In September 1850 the Compromise of 1850 became law, which meant that the Fugitive Slave Law was officially in effect throughout the United States. Harriet Beecher Stowe was angered by the passage of what she considered an unjust law. Her brother Henry Ward Beecher, a famous clergymen, was railing against the new law from his pulpit in New York, and Harriet, in a letter dated February 1, 1851, urged him to continue his fight in earnest: "I wish I had your chance—but next best to that is to have you have it—so fire away—give them no rest day or night."[14]

As a woman living in the mid–nineteenth century, Stowe had little opportunity to express her views in public. Her brother, though, could speak publicly on the social and moral issues of the day when he delivered his weekly sermon. If Stowe were a man, she could run for political office and air her views on slavery in the halls of her state legislature or in Congress. If she were a man, she could edit a newspaper and condemn slavery in ringing editorials. Women of the nineteenth century, however, were not afforded the opportunity to become ministers or lawmakers or newspaper editors. If Stowe wanted to speak out in public on the immorality of slavery, she would have to find another way to do so.

Stowe's sister-in-law, Isabella Beecher, had urged Stowe to use the power of her pen to attack the Fugitive Slave Law and the institution of slavery. So early in 1851, Stowe began to conceive of a project that would depict the evils of slavery. Early in January 1851, Stowe wrote to her brother Henry to describe the project: "I have begun a set of sketches in the National Era, to illustrate the cruelty of slavery: I call it *Uncle Tom's Cabin*."[15] Sometime after she conceived the idea for *Uncle Tom's Cabin*, Stowe claimed that she had a vision while attending services at the First Parish Church in Brunswick of a slave named Uncle Tom being beaten to death.

The previous summer, Stowe had written an article attacking the Fugitive Slave Law and had sent it to the *National Era*, a weekly abolitionist newspaper. Its editor, Gamaliel Bailey, had printed the article and had urged her to send more. Stowe had complied with the editor's request; and after writing three more articles for the paper, she had received a check for one hundred dollars and further encouragement. In March 1851 she wrote to Bailey to describe her new project to him; it would be "a series of sketches" about slavery that would be ready in two or three weeks and would "extend through three or four numbers." In that letter, Stowe also explained to Bailey why she had begun the antislavery sketches tentatively titled *Uncle Tom's Cabin*:

> Up to this year I have always felt that I had no particular call to meddle with this subject, and I dreaded to expose even my own mind to the full force of its exciting power. But I feel now that the time is come when even a woman or a child who can speak a word for freedom and humanity is bound to speak. . . . I hope every woman who can write will not be silent.[16]

The Opening of a Great Novel

The May 8, 1851, edition of the *National Era* contained an announcement about a forthcoming publication: "Week after next we propose to commence . . . the publication of a new story by Mrs. H. B. Stowe, the title of which will be, 'UNCLE TOM'S CABIN, OR THE MAN THAT WAS A THING.'" The first two chapters of Stowe's story, titled "In Which the Reader Is Introduced to a Man of Humanity" and "The Mother," appeared on the front page in the June 5 issue of the *National Era*.

The opening chapter of *Uncle Tom's Cabin* is set on the Shelby farm in Kentucky. Mr. and Mrs. Shelby are slave owners, but their slaves are treated decently. They receive enough to eat and are afforded clean and comfortable cabins in which to live. Mr. Shelby boasts of his most trusted slave, called Uncle Tom, who can be sent unescorted on errands in Cincinnati and return to the Shelby farm without any thoughts of escaping. But Mr. Shelby, described as "good-natured and kindly,"[17] is in great debt, and he is prepared to sell some of his slaves to a slave trader named Haley to acquire cash to satisfy his creditors. Against his wife's wishes, he decides to sell Uncle Tom and a boy named Harry, the son of a slave woman, Eliza Harris, Mrs. Shelby's personal servant. In the second chapter, Stowe introduces George Harris, Eliza's husband, a talented machinist who curses his condition of bondage and is anxious to escape from slavery.

An illustration from Uncle Tom's Cabin *depicts Eliza crossing the icy Ohio River to escape her captors.*

A Tale of Captivity and Escape

Stowe continued to supply the *National Era* with weekly installments detailing the fortunes of Uncle Tom and Eliza Harris. Tom is taken away by Haley. When Eliza hears that her son Harry is also to be sold to Haley, she takes the boy and escapes from the plantation during the night. When her absence is discovered the next morning, Haley appoints two associates to chase and apprehend the fugitive slave woman and her child. Though the captors employ search dogs to track her trail, they cannot reach Eliza until she is about to cross the Ohio River into the free state of Ohio. With the slave chasers on her heels, Eliza, with a young child in her arms, makes a dramatic crossing of the Ohio River across ice floes just as she is about to be captured.

Although Eliza reaches free territory in Ohio, she is not yet a free woman. The Fugitive Slave Law is in effect, which means that she can be apprehended in Ohio and sent back to bondage in Kentucky. But Eliza receives help at the Ohio home of Mr. and Mrs. Bird. Eliza, tired and hungry, knocks on their door at night imploring their help. At first, Mr. Bird, a state legislator, is reticent to assist runaway slaves because doing so is against the law. But Mrs. Bird intercedes, calling the Fugitive Slave Law "a shameful, wicked, abominable law"[18] that deserves to be broken. When Mr. Bird sees the worn out and helpless Eliza and her young child, he, too, realizes that Eliza deserves their help. Significantly, Mrs. Bird has lost a child to death, and she understands why the slave woman would choose to escape from her farm rather than lose her child.

The Birds direct Eliza and Harry to a Quaker village, a station on the Underground Railroad, where they are safely hidden and given food and clothing. At the Quaker village, Eliza is united with her husband, George, who has also made a daring escape from his plantation.

The Plight of Uncle Tom

Uncle Tom entertains no ideas of escape. He is a religious man, a devout Christian, who believes that God has chosen for him the life of a slave, and he reasons that escaping from slavery would violate God's wishes. When his wife, Aunt Chloe, condemns Haley for taking Tom away, Tom tells his wife, "Pray for them that 'spitefully use you, the good book says."[19] He is chained and placed in a wagon for a journey that will take him into the Deep South. Eventually he is put on a Mississippi riverboat.

Uncle Tom has begun a nightmarish journey into the Deep South, where slave owners are generally harsher than their counterparts in Kentucky, Virginia, and Missouri, the slave states that bordered the North. On his way downriver, Tom witnesses unspeakable acts of evil. He sees a mother and children separated at a slave auction. A

In this scene from Uncle Tom's Cabin, *Tom rescues Eva from the raging waters of the Mississippi River.*

slave woman named Lucy has her son sold at a riverport stop, and Lucy reacts by throwing herself overboard; she commits suicide by drowning rather than coping with her grief.

But Tom is, for a time, spared from a horrible fate. While on board the riverboat, Tom befriends a young white girl named Eva. When Eva slips and falls overboard, Tom jumps into the roaring Mississippi River to save her. As a reward, Augustine St. Clare, Eva's father, purchases Tom and brings him to his plantation in New Orleans, where Tom is treated kindly.

The Public's Reaction

Stowe continued to write in Brunswick, Maine, sending weekly installments of *Uncle Tom's Cabin* to the editor of the *National Era*. Her story, originally intended to be presented in full in four or five weekly editions, grew beyond that narrow scope. During the summer of 1851, Stowe was still supplying her editor, Gamaliel Bailey, with story material. The editor was worried that his newspaper's readers' interests would wane after several weeks, but the reading public eagerly devoured the story of Uncle Tom and Eliza Harris. *Uncle Tom's Cabin* became the main topic of discussion in literary circles. Ministers referred to the plight of Uncle Tom in their Sunday sermons. Politicians discussed the novel as well. Statesmen of the South condemned Stowe's story as an exaggeration; they said that slavery was not as harsh as Stowe depicted it in her novel. Northern statesmen used *Uncle Tom's Cabin* as an anthem in their crusade against slavery.

And Stowe continued to supply weekly installments. On a few occasions, she missed her publication deadline, and the *National Era* printed an apology to its readers with a promise that Stowe's remarkable story would be continued the following week. Those who followed the tale closely rushed to their mailboxes to retrieve the new edition and learn the fate of Stowe's characters.

Triumph for the Harris Family

In Stowe's story, George, Eliza, and Harry Harris successfully escape slavery's grasp. When the Harrises depart the safety of the Quaker village, they are trailed by slave chasers. George defends his family with pistols. He shoots and wounds Tom Loker, one of the men on his trail, and the others abandon the chase. Eventually the Harrises reach the safe haven of Canada, where slavery is legally prohibited. There, they become good Christians and productive citizens, free people never to experience bondage again.

By creating the Harris family, Stowe attempted to destroy some of the stereotypes that hampered African Americans of the

Abolitionists and runaway slaves fight off men sent to recapture runaway slaves.

mid–nineteenth century. Many Americans defended slavery because they considered African Americans to be unintelligent, uneducable people who were suited only for work in the fields. But Stowe makes George a skilled mechanic and engineer; she makes him literate as well. Some Americans justified the separation of slave families in auctions because slaves were supposedly unable to establish close family ties. But Eliza's love for her child and husband show her as a devoted mother and wife with great love for her family. In Stowe's novel, African Americans are fully human beings, capable of engaging in productive work, establishing family values, and becoming devout Christians.

Uncle Tom at the St. Clare Estate

Uncle Tom fares quite well at the St. Clare estate in New Orleans. Augustine St. Clare is a wealthy and kindly man who does not believe in overworking his slaves or punishing them severely. Uncle Tom works at the estate as St. Clare's foreman and is well treated, well fed, and well housed. He is allowed free time to read his Bible and play with little Eva St. Clare, who takes a liking to the man who saved her from drowning. Augustine eventually promises to grant Uncle Tom his freedom and allow him to return to Aunt Chloe and his own family on the

Uncle Tom is sent to the auction block after the death of his owner, Augustine St. Clare.

Shelby farm in Kentucky. When little Eva falls ill and dies, Uncle Tom is Augustine's closest comforter, and the two men become intimate friends.

But the forces of fate work against Uncle Tom. St. Clare, the man who promised Uncle Tom his freedom, is killed by a knife wound trying to break up a fight between two drunken men in a cafe. Marie St. Clare, Augustine's widow, decides to sell the plantation as well as all of its slaves. So instead of being given his freedom and sent home to Aunt Chloe, Uncle Tom is sent to the auction block, where he will be sold to the highest bidder and undoubtedly remain in bondage for the rest of his life.

Mean Simon Legree

Uncle Tom is sold to Simon Legree, a cruel and mean-spirited man who works his slaves to their deaths, then buys new ones to replace them. "I don't go for savin' niggers. Use up, and buy more, 's my way;—makes you less trouble, and I'm quite sure it comes cheaper in the end," he says. "When one nigger's dead, I buy another; and I find it comes cheaper and easier, every way."[20] Legree tries to prevent Uncle Tom from praying. "*I'm* your church now,"[21] he barks at Uncle Tom when the despondent slave attempts to find solace in his prayer book.

Legree's plantation is buried deep in the swamps of Louisiana. To reach the Legree farm, Uncle Tom and the other slaves whom Legree has purchased travel down a "wild, forsaken road, now winding through dreary pine barrens, where the wind whispered mournfully," with "doleful trees rising out of the slimy, spongy ground, hung with funereal black moss, while ever anon the loathsome form of the moccasin snake might be seen sliding among broken stumps and shattered branches that lay here and there, rotting in the water."[22] Legree's plantation is dirty and disheveled: "The ground [was] littered with broken pails, cobs of corn, and other slovenly remains. . . . What once was a large garden was now all grown over with weeds."[23] The plantation is a hellish wasteland, a sharp contrast to Uncle Tom's previous homes, the tidy Shelby farm and the opulent St. Clare estate.

At the Legree plantation, the slaves work hard in the fields picking cotton. When they tire or work too slowly to suit Legree, the slaves are severely beaten. Their food is meager; they sleep on the dirt floor in ramshackle cabins. Many of the slaves who have served for a time under Legree appear sickly and emaciated. After describing the deplorable conditions under which the Legree slaves labor, Stowe intrudes her own voice into her narrative, asking, "'Is God HERE?' Ah, how is it possible for the untaught heart to keep its faith, unswerving, in the face of dire misrule, and palpable, unrebuked injustice?"[24]

An illustration from Uncle Tom's Cabin *shows slaves conducting a prayer meeting.*

Saintly Uncle Tom

Despite these hardships, Uncle Tom labors with diligence and patience. He prays for relief but accepts his situation with fortitude. He is obedient to the evil Simon Legree, except in one circumstance. At one point, Legree orders Uncle Tom to whip a fellow slave named Lucy because she is too weak to work. Uncle Tom refuses to commit the sinful act of harming another human being, even though his master has commanded it. "No! no! no! my soul an't yours, Mas'r!" says Tom to Legree. "You haven't bought it,—ye can't buy it! It's been bought and paid for, by one that is able to keep it;—no matter, no matter, you can't harm me!"[25] Tom is brutally whipped for disobedience.

Uncle Tom plays the role of doctor and minister to his fellow slaves. He tries to provide comfort to those who have been beaten or who have become exhausted because of the overbearing workload. He urges his fellow slaves to pray and have faith that God will provide for them in the next world if they suffer on Earth. At Legree's plantation, even Uncle Tom's strong faith in God undergoes a severe challenge. But in a moment of despair, Uncle Tom suddenly regains his faith in God and experiences a rejuvenation of body and spirit. Legree tries but fails to break Uncle Tom's Christian faith. At one point, another slave urges Tom to kill Legree and free the entire plantation, but Tom refuses because his Christian duty is to love his enemies.

The Death of Uncle Tom

Uncle Tom would never dare to escape from slavery, even if he is held in bondage by the most wicked of masters, because Tom believes that it is his duty to obey his master. But two slaves on Legree's plantation, Cassy and Emmeline, plan to escape from Legree's hold and seek their freedom. Tom does not dissuade the two women from attempting to escape, and he even helps them achieve their goal. When Legree realizes that two of his slaves are missing, he goes to Uncle Tom and demands to know where the two runaways have gone. But Tom refuses to inform on his friends; for his act of disobedience, he receives an awful beating from two slaves acting on Legree's orders.

Tom is near death after such a terrible beating. He forgives the two slaves who beat him, and they convert to Christianity. While Uncle Tom is on his deathbed, a messenger arrives from the Shelby estate, young George Shelby, the son of Mr. Shelby, with enough money to purchase Tom and bring him home. But George Shelby is too late; he arrives in time only to hear some of Uncle Tom's last words: "O, Mas'r George! what a thing 't is to be a Christian!"[26] George Shelby expresses his wish that Legree will lose his soul to

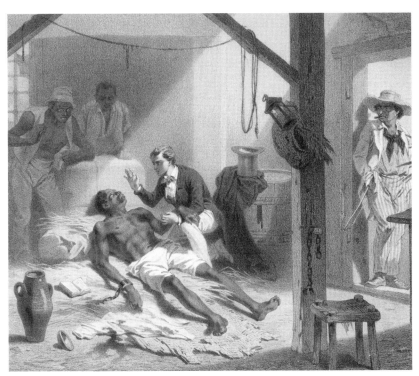

Young George Shelby offers Tom his freedom. Sadly, he is too late; Tom suffered a deadly beating ordered by his owner, Simon Legree.

hell for the killing of Uncle Tom, but Tom hopes that Legree will repent and save himself.

Uncle Tom loses his life, but his death gains freedom for all of the Shelby slaves. By this time, Mr. Shelby has died, and George is running the Shelby plantation. When George Shelby returns home with the news of Uncle Tom's death, he gathers the Shelby slaves and offers them their freedom. They can go their own ways or remain on the Shelby farm as paid workers. George tells his slaves that they can thank Uncle Tom for their freedom:

> "It was on his grave, my friends, that I resolved, before God, that I would never own another slave, while it is possible to free him; that nobody, through me, should ever run the risk of being parted from home and friends, and dying on a lonely plantation, as he died. So, when you rejoice in your freedom, think that you owe it to that good old soul, and pay it back in kindness to his wife and children. Think of your freedom, every time you see UNCLE TOM'S CABIN; and let it be the memorial to put you all in mind to follow in his steps, and be honest and faithful and Christian as he was."[27]

Stowe's Stirring Conclusion

Harriet Beecher Stowe ends her story of Uncle Tom with direct appeals to the reader. She urges American mothers to "pity those mothers that are constantly made childless by the American slave trade."[28] Stowe also appeals to the Christian church to take a more active role in the abolition of slavery. She urges Christians of the North to pray for those in bondage.

Stowe concludes her tale with a warning to both the North and the South:

> A day of grace is yet held out to us. Both North and South have been guilty before God; and the *Christian church* has a heavy account to answer. Not by combining together, to protect injustice and cruelty, and making a common capital of sin, is this Union to be saved,—but by repentance, justice and mercy; for, not surer is the eternal law by which the millstone sinks in the ocean, than that stronger law, by which injustice and cruelty shall bring on nations the wrath of Almighty God![29]

In a sense, Stowe is predicting the Civil War.

Publishing the Novel

The story of Uncle Tom ran in the *National Era* from June 5, 1851, through April 1, 1852, in a total of forty-one installments. Before the last chapters had been published, Stowe had negotiated a book contract with John P. Jewett and Company of Boston and Jewett, Procter, and Worthington of Cleveland to publish *Uncle Tom's Cabin* in two volumes, each running just more than three hundred pages. The book became available for sale in late March 1852.

Neither Stowe nor her publishers expected extraordinary sales; but published in book form, *Uncle Tom's Cabin* became an immediate runaway best-seller and broke all book sales records. On May 15, 1852, the publishers announced that 50,000 copies of the novel had already been sold. Orders were pouring in from all over the country, even from the South. Within one year, 300,000 copies had been sold in the United States. By early 1853 more than 1 million copies of *Uncle Tom's Cabin* had been sold in the United States and Great Britain. In the novel's first eighteen months of publication, Stowe received sixty thousand dollars in royalty payments, an extraordinary sum for an author of the 1850s.

Seemingly overnight, Harriet Beecher Stowe became a literary celebrity. Congratulatory messages poured in to the little-known

A nineteenth-century advertisement touts the best-seller Uncle Tom's Cabin *as "the greatest book of the age."*

writer living in Maine. Henry Wadsworth Longfellow, Frederick Douglass, John Greenleaf Whittier, Ralph Waldo Emerson, and other famous men and women of letters heaped praises on Stowe's great antislavery text. Stowe traveled the United States and Great Britain to promote her book.

But *Uncle Tom's Cabin* would become much more than a literary phenomenon. It would have an immediate and powerful impact on the great swirl of events during the decade before the American Civil War.

CHAPTER 3

The Sources of Stowe's Novel

Uncle Tom's Cabin is a highly original work of fiction. No antislavery work of its length and complexity had appeared earlier on the American literary landscape. Nonetheless, Harriet Beecher Stowe, in crafting her great novel, relied extensively on the religious and political ideas of her day. She also used the many abolitionist texts that had been published during the 1830s and 1840s, as sources for her tale of Uncle Tom. All authors are influenced by the ideas and books of their time. Stowe's ability to integrate into *Uncle Tom's Cabin* topics and issues of the mid–nineteenth-century marketplace of ideas remains one of the most remarkable features of her novel.

The Abolitionist Tradition

By the time Stowe began writing *Uncle Tom's Cabin* in 1851, a substantial body of abolitionist writing was readily available to the American public. William Lloyd Garrison had begun his abolitionist newspaper, the *Liberator*, in 1831, and his ideas and the ideas of other abolitionists who wrote for his paper were known throughout the United States. In 1839 Theodore Weld, a colleague of Lyman Beecher at Lane Theological Seminary in Cincinnati, had published *American Slavery as It Is: Testimony of a Thousand Witnesses*. This text, which consisted largely of articles from Southern newspapers, advertisements for runaway slaves, and similar documents, attempted to expose the evils of slavery by showing how the institution was presented in the South. Weld's book was widely read in the North and carefully examined by all members of the Beecher family.

Stowe absorbed the ideas and arguments of mid–nineteenth-century abolitionists. In addition, two slave narratives inspired Stowe as she wrote *Uncle Tom's Cabin* and provided her with important background material for her novel—Frederick Douglass's *Narrative of the Life of Frederick Douglass, an American Slave*, published in 1845, and Josiah Henson's *The Life of Josiah Henson*, published in 1849.

Narrative of the Life of Frederick Douglass

Frederick Douglass's first autobiography—he would publish two more in later years—narrates a compelling story. Douglass was born a slave on a Maryland farm. He never knew who his father was—though he was almost certain that his father was a white man—and he was separated from his mother at an earlier age. Throughout his childhood, Douglass witnessed the harshness of slaves' lives. He saw slaves brutally beaten for minor infractions, and he heard reports of slave owners actually murdering their slaves for disobedience. Douglass himself experienced severe beatings when he failed to perform to perfection a duty that his master had assigned him.

Slaves were sometimes punished with death for disobedience.

Yet throughout his childhood and young adulthood, Douglass kept alive the hope that he would somehow escape from slavery's clutches during his lifetime. At an early age, he realized that learning to read and write—skills that most slaves were not taught—would put him on the road to freedom, and he worked hard to become a self-taught reader and writer. When he was about twenty years old, Douglass was able to

The London Anti-Slavery Convention of 1840

The American women's rights movement of the mid–nineteenth century received its jump start from an antislavery convention held in London in 1840. A large group of American women, including women's rights activists like Elizabeth Cady Stanton and Lucretia Mott, arrived at the convention intending to take an active part in its proceedings. All were members of antislavery societies in the United States, and they were eager to discuss their abolitionist efforts with antislavery delegates from Great Britain and Europe who would be attending the convention. But on the first day of the convention, a fierce debate ensued on whether female delegates should be seated at the convention. Some male delegates, such as William Lloyd Garrison, spoke up in defense of the women, but the debate ended with the female delegates being excluded from the convention. Elizabeth Cady Stanton would later refer to the men who barred women from the convention as narrow-minded bigots.

When they returned to the United States, the women who were barred from participating in the convention kept in touch with each other by letters. From this correspondence came the idea for a convention devoted to women's rights to be held in the United States, in Seneca Falls, New York. The Seneca Falls Women's Convention of 1848 was the first conference on women's rights in American history.

Women's rights activist Elizabeth Cady Stanton was also involved in the antislavery movement.

escape from slavery and move to the North, where he met William Lloyd Garrison and became an eloquent voice in the abolitionist movement.

Douglass records the compelling story of his bondage and escape in *Narrative of the Life of Frederick Douglass*, and Stowe used that text as a source for *Uncle Tom's Cabin*. Douglass was the model for Stowe's character George Harris, the highly intelligent slave who despises slavery and vows to escape its grasp. Like Douglass, Harris flees from his master, escapes to the North under the cover of a disguise, and, upon achieving his freedom, becomes an eloquent antislavery spokesman.

Josiah Henson, an obedient slave who bypassed an opportunity to escape out of loyalty to his master, was Stowe's model for Uncle Tom.

The Life of Josiah Henson

Josiah Henson was a slave born in Maryland in 1789. As a young man, he attended a religious camp meeting and immediately thereafter became a devout Christian. He was an obedient slave who believed that he had a duty to submit to his master. At one point in his life, Henson's master decided to move from Maryland to Kentucky, and he ordered Henson to lead a group of slaves, without supervision, on that long trek. En route to Kentucky, Henson and his fellow slaves crossed into Ohio, a free state, but Henson decided not to seek freedom. For him, running away from his master, who had trusted him to journey unsupervised, would be dishonorable.

Henson did eventually escape from slavery, but only after his master had cheated him out of the money that Henson had saved to purchase his freedom. After reaching safety in Canada, Henson became a Methodist minister. He traveled widely, preaching and speaking of his experiences as a slave.

Stowe used Henson as a model for Uncle Tom. Like Henson, Stowe's Uncle Tom is a religious man who remains obedient to his master. Also like Henson, Uncle Tom can be trusted to perform a duty in a free state and not try to seek his freedom by escaping. Unlike Henson, however,

The Great Awakening

In the 1730s and 1740s, a great religious revival spread across the American colonies. This religious revival would
become known as the Great Awakening.

The Great Awakening began with a handful of
Protestant ministers who were powerful sermoniz-
ers—William and Gilbert Tennent of New Jersey,
Jonathan Edwards of Connecticut, and George Whitefield of
Georgia. These ministers gained huge followings, both in their
own congregations and throughout the American colonies. They traveled throughout the colonies, and their fiery sermons were published
and distributed widely.

Great Awakening ministers did not preach the same message, but
common themes emerged from their sermons. All ministers emphasized the omnipotent power of God, human beings' tendency toward
sin and their inability to save themselves from eternal damnation
without the grace of God, and the belief that the end of the world and
Judgment Day were close at hand. Typical of the sermons of the Great
Awakening was Jonathan Edwards's "Sinners in the Hands of an
Angry God," first delivered in 1741, in which he depicts humankind
as a loathsome spider, ready for eternal punishment, being held by
God over a pit of fire.

The ministers of the Second Great Awakening, which took place
during Harriet Beecher Stowe's lifetime, rejected the harsh message
of the preachers of the Great Awakening. These ministers of the
mid–nineteenth century emphasized God's willingness to forgive even
the most sinful human beings if they were prepared to confess their
sins and reform themselves.

Uncle Tom is never released from slavery's grasp. Henson's story ends
in triumph, with Henson a free man, a minister preaching the Gospel;
Stowe's tale of Uncle Tom ends in tragedy, with his painful death at the
hands of Simon Legree.

The Second Great Awakening

In the 1820s and 1830s, a religious revival later known as the Second
Great Awakening swept across America, and Stowe was certainly influenced by it. Theologians and ministers associated with this movement challenged the rigid religious doctrines of the Calvinists,
whose beliefs took hold in America in the seventeenth century. The
Calvinists believed that a powerful God controlled human destiny,

that human beings lacked the free will to achieve salvation unless salvation were predestined by God. Those who challenged Calvinist doctrine argued that human beings, even sinners, could be saved if they reformed themselves. Stowe's father, Reverend Lyman Beecher, was associated with the Second Great Awakening. Ministers like Reverend Beecher believed that they could function as instruments of God who could enable the sinful to repent and earn God's grace and forgiveness.

The religious principles of the Second Great Awakening were the backbone of many mid–nineteenth-century social movements. Reverend Beecher and other ministers believed that if an individual could reform himself or herself and earn God's grace, then surely society could reform itself and receive God's blessing. Both the temperance movement and the abolitionist movement were fueled by this belief. Temperance people, who opposed the sale and use of alcoholic beverages, believed that an individual drunkard could quit drinking and save himself; they also believed that society could purge itself of the social ills created by alcoholism—wife and child abuse, homelessness, unemployment—if it outlawed alcohol. Likewise, abolitionists saw slavery as a serious sin against God; but if America rid itself of slavery, it could again receive God's blessings.

Uncle Tom's Cabin offers a plea to America to abolish slavery. Stowe depicts slavery as an offense that has displeased God and must be eradicated or else God's wrath will come down upon the nation. She concludes *Uncle Tom's Cabin* by asserting that "both North and South have been guilty before God" and that the "injustice and cruelty" of slavery "shall bring on nations the wrath of Almighty God."[30] The United States can save itself from this fate, however, if it rejects slavery. Stowe also suggests in her novel that individuals can be reformed if they denounce slavery. Sam

Reverend Lyman Beecher, Stowe's father, believed that slavery was a serious sin against God.

and Quimbo, the two slaves who, acting on orders from Simon Legree, torment and abuse Uncle Tom, are converted by Tom on his deathbed. Uncle Tom even urges Simon Legree to repent and change his evil ways to avoid God's condemnation, though Legree rejects Tom's message.

The American Romantics

Stowe published *Uncle Tom's Cabin* at a time when the American literary marketplace was dominated by writers who would later become known as the American Romantics. The Romantics included the essayists Ralph Waldo Emerson, Margaret Fuller, and Henry David Thoreau; the novelists Nathaniel Hawthorne and Herman Melville; and the poets William Cullen Bryant, Henry Wadsworth Longfellow, and John Greenleaf Whittier.

The Romantics were a diffuse group of writers, but they shared a common ideology and addressed common themes and issues in their writing. Most Romantics believed in the healing power of the natural world; they embraced the idea that an individual could escape the follies and miseries of humankind by experiencing nature—the forests, the seashore, the rivers. They were skeptical of formal institutions such as the church and the government. The Romantics were nonconformists; they believed that individuals—not the church or government—must determine for themselves right from wrong. Therefore, they frequently challenged the laws of the state and the tenets of the church. The Romantics also condemned the commercialism and materialism that had become a part of mid–nineteenth-century American culture; they believed that Americans had become too obsessed with making money and had sacrificed important spiritual values in the process.

Thoreau's writings present many of the ideas of

American Romantic writer, Henry David Thoreau, published Walden *in 1854, recounting his two years at Walden Pond.*

the American Romantics. His most famous book, *Walden*, published in 1854, records his two-year stay in a cabin that he built for himself at Walden Pond outside of Concord, Massachusetts. Thoreau had found life in Concord too confining, and his time at Walden Pond was an experiment in self-sufficiency—to determine whether he could survive on his own in the natural world away from the hustle and bustle of American society.

"Civil Disobedience"

Walden was published after *Uncle Tom's Cabin*, but Stowe might have been familiar with the ideas expressed in Thoreau's earlier writings, particularly the themes articulated in his most famous essay, "Civil Disobedience." In that essay Thoreau questions the ability of the government to make just laws that will benefit American citizens. He calls the American government "a *slave's* government" that enacts unjust laws, such as those that defend the institution of slavery. Thoreau urges his readers not to cultivate a respect for law, but to develop a respect for what is right: "The only obligation which I have a right to assume, is to do at any time what I think right." Thoreau advises his readers to break unjust laws rather than to obey them: "If it [the law] is of such a nature that it requires you to be the agent of injustice to another, then, I say, break the law. Let your life be a counter friction to stop the machine. What I have to do is to see, at any rate, that I do not lend myself to the wrong which I condemn."[31] Thoreau himself once spent a night in jail for refusing to pay a tax that he felt was unjust.

Stowe incorporates some of Thoreau's ideas in the chapter of *Uncle Tom's Cabin* that is set in the home of the Birds. Eliza Harris and her young son, Harry, arrive at the Birds' home after they have crossed the Ohio River and escaped from the slave chasers employed by Haley, the slave trader who has purchased Harry and Uncle Tom. Before Eliza's arrival, Mr. and Mrs. Bird have a discussion regarding the Fugitive Slave Law, which Mr. Bird, a state senator, has been discussing in the state legislature. Mrs. Bird is astonished that her husband should support the passage of such a law: "Is it true that they have been passing a law forbidding people to give meat and drink to those poor colored folks that come along? I heard they were talking of some such law, but I didn't think any Christian legislature would pass it!" When Mr. Bird concedes that he voted for such a law, Mrs. Bird, echoing Thoreau, declares, "You ought to be ashamed, John! Poor, homeless, houseless creatures! It's a shameful, wicked, abominable law, and I'll break it, for one, the first time I get a chance; and I hope I *shall* have the chance, I do!"[32] Mrs. Bird gets the chance to break the law, and does, moments later when Eliza Harris knocks on the door.

A Culture of Money

Like Thoreau and other Romantics, Stowe condemned mid–nineteenth-century American society's emphasis on earning money and accumulating wealth. At Walden Pond, Thoreau led a spartan existence in a small cabin with only a few pieces of furniture. He owned only a few articles of clothing. He worked only several weeks per year because he had no desire to make money and accumulate wealth.

The worst villains in *Uncle Tom's Cabin* are those whose only desire in life is to make money. Haley, the slave trader who purchases Uncle Tom at the start of the novel, senses that slavery is morally wrong, but slave trading provides him with a good income, so he will

An illustration from Uncle Tom's Cabin *portrays the cruelest of slavery villains, Simon Legree, threatening Tom with a whip.*

not give it up. "I'll say this now, I al'ays meant to drive my trade so as to make money on 't, *fust and foremost*," he says. When he makes enough money from slave trading—"when I've got matters tight and snug"—he promises "to tend to my soul."[33] Haley and Simon Legree are the epitome of men obsessed with money; they have sacrificed their souls in an attempt to accumulate wealth.

Augustine St. Clare, the New Orleans aristocrat who owns Uncle Tom for a time and treats him kindly, speaks for Stowe when he discusses the reason for slavery's existence. Slavery exists mainly to bring wealth to Southern planters:

> "He [the slave owner] says that there can be no high civilization without enslavement of the masses, either nominal or real. There must be, he says, a lower class, given up to physical toil and confined to an animal nature; and a higher one thereby acquires leisure and wealth for a more expanded intelligence and improvement, and becomes the directing soul of the lower."[34]

In St. Clare's and Stowe's view, slavery is an evil closely linked to American society's emphasis on making money and acquiring wealth.

The Mid–Nineteenth-Century Feminists

In *Uncle Tom's Cabin*, Stowe also enunciated the ideas of mid–nineteenth-century American feminists. By this time a very active women's movement was occurring in the United States. American women had few political rights, social privileges, or economic opportunities. By the 1840s an articulate group of American women—including Elizabeth Cady Stanton, Angelina and Sarah Grimké, and Lucretia Mott—had begun to protest the conditions under which most American women lived. Woman could not vote or run for public office or even speak in public on political issues. They could not own property; any property that they acquired would become their husband's property. Colleges and universities were closed to women, as were careers that required an advanced education.

In July 1848 the first women's rights convention in American history was held in Seneca Falls, New York, to address these issues. The convention attendees adopted the Declaration of Sentiments, which addressed the economic, educational, social, and political needs of mid–nineteenth-century American women. Written in the style of Thomas Jefferson's Declaration of Independence, the Declaration of Sentiments boldly asserts "that all men and women are created equal; that they are endowed by their Creator with certain inalienable

The first women's rights convention in Seneca Falls, New York, addressed political, social, and economic issues concerning women.

rights, that among these rights are life, liberty, and the pursuit of happiness." The document declares that "the history of mankind is a history of repeated injuries and usurpations on the part of man toward women, having in direct object the establishment of an absolute tyranny over her." These repeated injuries include denying women their "inalienable right to the elective franchise," leaving women "without representation in the halls of legislation," taking from women "all right in property," depriving women of "nearly all the profitable employments" and "a thorough education," and delegating women to "a subordinate position" in both "Church and State."[35]

"A Powerfully Feminist Book"

The literary critic Ann Douglas properly calls *Uncle Tom's Cabin* "a powerfully feminist book."[36] The novel incorporates many of the convictions of the mid–nineteenth-century American feminists. In the opening chapters, for example, Stowe depicts, through Mrs. Shelby, the powerless position that women held in the American family. Mr. Shelby sells Uncle Tom and Harry, the son of Eliza, Mrs. Shelby's personal servant, without even consulting his wife. When Mrs. Shelby hears about the transaction, she protests vigorously to her husband, but Mr. Shelby dismisses her appeal. "I'm sorry, very sorry, Emily," he says. "I'm sorry this takes hold of you so; but it will do no good. The fact is, Emily, the thing's done; the bills are already signed and in Haley's hand; and you must be thankful it is no worse."[37]

In a similar scene, Senator Bird tries to dismiss his wife's opposition to the Fugitive Slave Law. Mrs. Bird is politically impotent; she cannot vote or speak in public on her objection to that law. But Stowe imbues

This scene from Uncle Tom's Cabin *depicts Mrs. Bird convincing her husband, Senator Bird, that refusing to aid runaway slaves is morally wrong.*

Mrs. Bird with a feminist's verve and tenacity; she refuses to calmly accept her husband's argument. She convinces him that refusing to aid a runaway slave is morally wrong. When Eliza Harris knocks on the door of the Birds' home, Senator Bird is as anxious as Mrs. Bird to provide her with assistance.

The scene in *Uncle Tom's Cabin* that best reveals Stowe's feminist leanings takes place in the chapter titled "The Quaker Settlement." Eliza Harris is taken to a Quaker village for safe hiding on her journey to Canada. She stays in the home of Rachel Halliday, which Stowe presents as a utopia, a perfect world. The Halliday family members cooperate in running the household: "Everything went on so sociably, so quietly, so harmoniously, in the great kitchen."[38] The Hallidays treat white and black people equally; George and Eliza Harris eat at the same table as the members of the Halliday family. Significantly, the Halliday home is matriarchal; it is headed by a woman, Rachel Halliday, who sits at the head of the table at dinnertime and holds court in the living room while sitting in her rocking chair. In Stowe's view, the world might be a better place if it were ruled by women like Rachel Halliday.

Harriet Beecher Stowe was a woman who was aware of the political, social, and economic issues of her time. The great issues of the day were discussed in the Beecher and Stowe households. Moreover, Stowe was an active reader; through books, she remained keenly attuned to the intellectual climate of mid–nineteenth-century America. Her greatest novel, *Uncle Tom's Cabin*, presents to her readers an active discussion of many of the major issues of her time.

The War to End American Slavery

4

During the decade following the publication of *Uncle Tom's Cabin*, the United States became a nation bitterly divided. Until 1850 the North and the South had been able to settle their differences over slavery through political compromise; the Missouri Compromise of 1820 and the Compromise of 1850 helped to maintain the Union and avert civil war. After 1850, however, the time for compromise appeared to have ended, as the North and the South moved farther apart politically and closer toward war.

Perhaps President Abraham Lincoln was exaggerating when he suggested, in 1862, that Harriet Beecher Stowe's great antislavery novel had caused the Civil War. Stowe's book did not on its own ignite the American catastrophe that occurred from 1861 through 1865; other people and events moved the United States on the course toward civil war. But *Uncle Tom's Cabin* contributed in a significant way to the national debate over slavery during the 1850s that resulted in the most terrible war in American history. As Civil War historian James M. McPherson asserts, "It is not possible to measure precisely the political influence of *Uncle Tom's Cabin*. One can quantify its sales but cannot point to votes that it changed or laws that it inspired. Yet few contemporaries doubted its power."[39]

Uncle Tom's Cabin *was condemned in the South, where one newspaper editor called Stowe a "vile wretch in petticoats."*

The Impact of *Uncle Tom's Cabin*

Hundreds of thousands of Americans read *Uncle Tom's Cabin*, and few were unaffected by it. In the South, the novel was almost unanimously condemned. For example, the

The Civil War Amendments

The Thirteenth Amendment to the
U.S. Constitution outlawed slavery,
but it did nothing to guarantee that former slaves would enjoy the rights and privileges of American citizenship. In fact, in the
aftermath of the Civil War the Southern states passed
laws and ordinances to restrict the freedom of former
slaves. They could not vote, run for public office, or apply for
jobs designated for white workers, and they could be arrested for
vagrancy and given a stiff prison term if they left their old plantations.
Freed slaves who committed minor crimes were subjected to extraor-
dinarily severe punishments.

In an attempt to deal with the problems of former slaves, Congress
proposed the Fourteenth and Fifteenth Amendments to the Constitution. The Fourteenth Amendment, which was adopted in 1868, stipulated that all persons born in the United States would be citizens,
regardless of race or previous condition of servitude, and all citizens
would be entitled to equal protection under the law. In 1870 the Fifteenth Amendment became part of the Constitution. This amendment stipulated that no state could deny the voting rights of U.S.
citizens.

For almost one hundred years, African Americans living in the
South did not enjoy the rights guaranteed by the Fourteenth and Fifteenth Amendments. Not until the civil rights movement of the 1950s
and 1960s were citizenship and voting rights gradually extended to
African Americans in the South.

editor of the *Southern Literary Messenger* damned the novel and called
Harriet Beecher Stowe a "vile wretch in petticoats."[40] Southern slave
holders defended their institution more arduously in the face of Stowe's
critique. In the antislavery North, the reviews of *Uncle Tom's Cabin*
were overwhelmingly positive. More important, however, was the
novel's impact on ordinary citizens.

Letters, diaries, and journals of the 1850s attest to the ways in
which Stowe's novel affected its readers. A typical response is one
recorded in a letter sent to Stowe by a reader who had just completed
the novel:

> I sat up last night long after one o'clock, reading and finish-
> ing "Uncle Tom's Cabin." I *could not* leave it any more than I
> could have left a dying child; nor could I restrain an almost

hysterical sobbing for an hour after I laid my head upon my pillow. I thought I was a thorough-going Abolitionist before, but your book has awakened so strong a feeling of indignation and compassion, that I seem never to have had *any* feeling on this subject till now. But what can we do? Alas! alas! what *can* we do?[41]

Many Northerners who had previously been tolerant of slavery turned bitterly against the institution after reading Stowe's moving story of Uncle Tom. Abolitionists who read the novel—especially clergymen, politicians, writers, editors, and others who had the public's ear—doubled their efforts, creating an environment in which further compromise on slavery would become politically impossible.

Bleeding Kansas

The first shots of the inevitable conflict were fired on the western frontier in Kansas. Since the 1830s, pioneers in search of cheap land had been moving westward from Illinois, Iowa, Kentucky, and Missouri to the Kansas-Nebraska Territory. By 1854 this territory was ready to apply for statehood, and the inevitable debate began on whether the territory should be admitted to the Union as a free state or as a slave state. Senator Stephen Douglas of Illinois proposed that the large Kansas-Nebraska Territory be divided into two states and that the citizens of each state be allowed to decide, by a vote, whether slavery would be legal or prohibited. Douglas's concept of letting citizens of a state or territory decide on the matter of slavery became known as popular sovereignty. Southerners supported the idea because it meant that the local population, not the federal government, would decide whether slavery would be legal in an area. Most antislavery Northerners opposed popular sovereignty because it meant that slavery could be further extended.

Douglas's proposal prevailed. After an extended and bitter debate, the Kansas-Nebraska Act became law in May 1854. Kansas would be the first of the two territories to decide on the issue of slavery, and both proslavery and antislavery settlers began streaming into Kansas to cast their ballots in the forthcoming vote. Not long afterward, violence erupted between the two factions, and Kansas became known as "Bleeding Kansas." Only the commitment of federal troops to the area to maintain peace prevented a full-scale civil war from breaking out.

African American Soldiers

At the start of the Civil War, African Americans were prohibited from serving in the U.S. military. During the war, civil rights leaders like Frederick Douglass began pressuring President Abraham Lincoln to allow African Americans to join the federal army to participate in the war to end slavery. At first, Lincoln was reticent to allow African Americans to join the military. When he issued the Emancipation Proclamation on January 1, 1863, however, Lincoln announced a new War Department policy to allow African Americans to join the federal army and navy.

Thousands of young African American men—freed slaves and Northern freemen—answered Lincoln's call. In the beginning, African American soldiers performed only menial tasks such as loading ammunition wagons, guarding camps and bridges, and digging graves; but by the summer of 1863, African American soldiers were ready for combat. In June a black regiment saw action at a skirmish at Liliken's Bend, Louisiana, and gave a good account of itself in battle. In July a black regiment, the Fifty-fourth Massachusetts, led the Union charge on Fort Wagner in South Carolina. The attack against a strongly defended Confederate position was not well planned, but the regiment impressed the entire North with its valor. Unflinchingly, the African American troops, who were commanded by a white officer named Colonel Robert Gould Shaw, marched into Confederate cannon and gunfire. The regiment suffered 40 percent casualties in the engagement, but not one soldier failed in his duty, dispelling the notions of those who thought that black troops could not be disciplined and would not demonstrate courage on the battlefield.

African Americans line up after being admitted into the military.

64

The *Dred Scott* Case

A U.S. Supreme Court decision on a slave named Dred Scott added to the escalating tensions between the North and the South. Scott, a slave living in Missouri, had accompanied his master, John Emerson, to the free state of Illinois, where they resided for a short time. After they moved back to Missouri, Emerson died, and his widow claimed ownership of Scott. At that point, Scott sued for his freedom, claiming that he had become a free man while living in Illinois. Mrs. Emerson maintained that Scott remained her late husband's property even though Scott had lived in a free state for a time. Scott lost his case in federal court, but he appealed to the U.S. Supreme Court, which has the right to overturn the decisions of lower courts.

Dred Scott

In 1857 the Supreme Court decided Scott's case, ruling that Scott would remain a slave, the property of Mrs. Emerson. Chief Justice Roger B. Taney, writing the majority opinion for the Court, asserted that Scott was not a U.S. citizen; hence he had no rights under the U.S. Constitution. According to Chief Justice Taney, Scott was merely a piece of property, like a horse or a wagon. Emerson could take his property to any state, and that property would remain in his ownership. Chief Justice Taney stated,

> The right of property in a slave is distinctly and expressly affirmed in the Constitution. The right to traffic in it, like an ordinary article of merchandise and property, was guaranteed to the citizens of the United States, in every State that might desire it. . . . And the Government in express terms is pledged to protect it in all future time, if the slave escapes from the owner.[42]

Chief Justice Taney's decision in the case of *Dred Scott* offered one more controversial ruling. Taney concluded that Congress had no

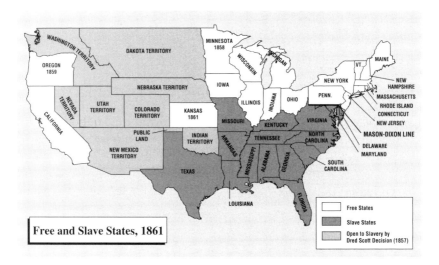

Free and Slave States, 1861

Free States

Slave States

Open to Slavery by
Dred Scott Decision (1857)

right to outlaw slavery in any state or territory; that decision was left solely to the local population. Thus, Taney's decision rendered the Compromise of 1820 unconstitutional because it had outlawed slavery in U.S. territories above the latitude mark of 36°30´.

Reaction to the *Dred Scott* Decision

Southerners applauded the Supreme Court's decision. They had always considered their slaves to be private property, and they had always opposed any attempt by the federal government to outlaw slavery in any U.S. state or territory.

Antislavery Northerners condemned Chief Justice Taney and the Court's ruling. They considered African Americans, even those held in bondage, American citizens who possessed all the rights named in the U.S. Constitution. Furthermore, abolitionists feared the implications of Taney's decision. If Congress had no right to regulate slavery, then slavery could spread unchecked across the United States. And if one slave owner, John Emerson, could bring one slave into a free state and maintain ownership of that slave, what would prevent a slave owner from bringing one hundred slaves into a free state and maintaining ownership of them? How could the federal government prevent a Southern slave owner from moving his hundred slaves to Massachusetts, a free state, and operating a farm there with slave labor?

One Northerner who was particularly troubled by the implications of the *Dred Scott* case was Abraham Lincoln, an Illinois politician who had recently joined the newly formed Republican Party, which was dedicated to the position that slavery should not spread to new states and territories. Lincoln saw the day when the Supreme Court would deliver a follow-up decision to the *Dred Scott* case that would make slavery lawful in every state of the Union.

John Brown's Raid

As the rift between the North and the South grew greater, an incident occurred in Harpers Ferry, Virginia, that seemed to make war between the two factions inevitable. John Brown, an abolitionist from Ohio who had waged war against proslavery settlers in Kansas in 1856, attempted to strike a blow against the "Slave Power," the slaveholding Southern planters and the politicians who supported them. Brown feared that, in the wake of the *Dred Scott* decision, the Slave

Chief Justice Roger B. Taney (pictured) decided that Dred Scott was not a U.S. citizen and therefore was not entitled to rights under the Constitution.

Power was gaining energy that would result in the legalization of slavery throughout the United States. Brown had been brought up to believe that slavery was a sin against God, and he was devoted to erasing slavery from the American landscape. In the wake of the *Dred Scott* decision, he had little faith that slavery could be uprooted through the courts or through legislative initiatives. In Brown's view, something more drastic would have to be done.

Early in 1858 Brown began implementing a plan that he had originally conceived during his days in Kansas. He planned to ignite a massive slave uprising by arming slaves who would revolt against their masters and free themselves. The revolution would begin with a few dozen slaves but would spread throughout the entire South, eventually ridding America of slavery forever. By the summer of 1859, Brown had solicited funds for his enterprise from wealthy and influential abolitionists, and he had begun to assemble a small force to carry out the plan.

Brown's plan centered on Harpers Ferry, a small industrial town on the Virginia side of the Potomac River that held a U.S. weapons arsenal. Weapons were made in a Harpers Ferry munitions factory and stored in nearby warehouses for use in a national emergency. Brown reasoned that if he captured the arsenal and warehouses, which were not heavily defended, he could arm hundreds of slaves on

John Brown and a group of twenty-one followers seized control of an arsenal in Harpers Ferry. The rebellion lasted only forty-eight hours before Robert E. Lee and his troops quelled it.

nearby plantations. Those slaves could liberate themselves and attack other plantations. The rebellion would eventually encompass all of Virginia and adjacent Maryland, then spread farther until slaves were rebelling throughout the entire South.

On the evening of October 16, 1859, Brown and his force of twenty-one abolitionist crusaders stole into Harpers Ferry, cut telegraph lines, apprehended the sentries who guarded weapons warehouses, and took control of the town. Brown also sent several men to nearby plantations to liberate the slaves and urge them to join his rebellion.

But early the next morning, Brown's plan began to unravel. A railroad train passed through Harpers Ferry, and its conductor spread the news of Brown's raid. Soon, nearby Virginia militiamen were marching toward Harpers Ferry. When they arrived, they shot and captured several of Brown's recruits. The next day a battalion of U.S. Marines under the command of Colonel Robert E. Lee arrived in Harpers Ferry. By this time Brown and his remaining men were trapped in a firehouse. Lee's men rushed Brown's makeshift fortress, wounding and capturing Brown and killing several of his men. His grand rebellion had lasted less than forty-eight hours.

The Trial of John Brown

Brown was indicted for treason and murder. The Virginia authorities who held Brown hoped for a quick trial and execution, but Brown did not go quietly to the gallows. His trial made front-page news in newspapers throughout the United States. His statements in court were quoted in full, and he became the subject of editorials, speeches, and sermons. Southerners condemned Brown as a traitor and murderer, a Satan who had tried to ignite a slave rebellion that would destroy the economy of the entire South. To abolitionists, however, Brown was a hero, a saint, a martyr who was willing to lay down his life to rid America of slavery. Henry David Thoreau, the philosopher and writer from Concord, Massachusetts, saluted Brown as a hero who gave his life to help the cause of the oppressed. Harriet Beecher Stowe, traveling in Italy when Brown was executed, described Brown in a letter as "a brave good man who calmly gave his life up to a noble effort for human freedom, and died in a way that is better than the most successful selfish life."[43]

Brown was found guilty of all charges and was hanged on December 2, 1859, but he was not quickly forgotten. On the day of his death, church bells throughout the North tolled for a fallen martyr, and abolitionist ministers, politicians, writers, and orators eulogized Brown in passionate speeches and essays. In Northern churches and at antislavery rallies,

John Brown, found guilty of treason and murder, walks to his execution.

abolitionists began singing a song called "John Brown's Body," whose chorus intoned, "John Brown's body lies a-moulderin' in the grave, / But his soul is marching on!"

On a Course Toward War

John Brown's raid put the United States on a course toward civil war. Even Congress seemed at war. Southern congressmen accused their Northern counterparts of masterminding Brown's raid at Harpers Ferry and thereby igniting a rebellion designed to eradicate slavery and destroy the South. Southerners speculated that dozens of other Northern abolitionists were planning schemes like Brown's. Northern congressmen, in turn, reiterated the evils of slavery and asserted that

Frederick Stowe: Casualty of the Civil War

Harriet Beecher Stowe's son Frederick participated in the Civil War. He was wounded in the Battle of Gettysburg and never completely recovered. Frederick Stowe became a casualty of the war that his mother helped ignite with her antislavery novel.

Frederick was born in 1840. He was almost twenty-one years old when Fort Sumter fell, beginning the Civil War. In May 1861 he answered President Abraham Lincoln's call for seventy-five thousand volunteers to join the federal army to put down the Southern rebellion. Frederick joined Company A of the First Massachusetts volunteer infantry and saw his first action in July at the Battle of Bull Run, a disastrous defeat for the Union army.

For the next two years, Frederick saw little action, as his regiment was assigned to duty at Fort Runyon, one of the garrisons protecting Washington, D.C., from a Rebel attack. Frederick complained to his mother about the monotony of garrison duty, and she interceded on his behalf. She contacted an old family friend, Brigadier General Adolph von Steinwehr, a division commander in the Army of the Potomac. In a short time, Lieutenant Frederick Stowe was assigned to General von Steinwehr as an aide-de-camp.

General von Steinwehr's division was one of the first to engage in combat during the Battle of Gettysburg. After the first day of fighting, General von Steinwehr's troops were positioned on Cemetery Hill, near the center of the Union line. During the Confederate artillery barrage preceding Major General George Pickett's fatal charge into the center of the Union position, Frederick was wounded near the ear with a shell fragment. He spent the rest of the war recovering from that wound.

Before the war, Frederick had experienced problems with alcohol, which was particularly embarrassing to his family because the Stowes were temperance people. During the war, Frederick mostly avoided alcohol's temptation. After the war, however, Frederick, depressed by his injury, began drinking again. He tried several times to deal with his problem by attending an alcohol rehabilitation center and by praying earnestly for his recovery. But he could not break his dependency on alcohol.

Frederick disappeared in 1871. As a last desperate attempt to break his alcohol dependency, he had traveled to San Francisco to embark on a Pacific Ocean cruise. Frederick never boarded the ship and was never heard from again.

a more widespread slave revolt was inevitable. During one session of the House of Representatives a few days after Brown's execution, a Mississippi congressman attacked Representative Thaddeus Stevens, an abolitionist from Pennsylvania, with a bowie knife. A murder was avoided only because Stevens's Republican colleagues were able to apprehend the knife-wielding Mississippian. Congressmen began carrying guns and knives in the halls of Congress, ready for use if a congressional debate turned violent.

Clearly, the days of compromise between the North and the South were over. The bitter national debate over slavery, exacerbated by the publication of *Uncle Tom's Cabin*, was ready to explode into full scale war.

The Election of 1860

After John Brown's raid, the next battle between Northerners and Southerners would be waged during the presidential election of 1860. Abolitionists in the North were eager to nominate a presidential candidate dedicated to the elimination of slavery; meanwhile, Southerners wanted a candidate sympathetic to their desire to see slavery extended.

Meeting in Chicago, the six-year-old Republican Party, which was pledged to limiting the spread of slavery, united behind Abraham Lincoln of Illinois as its candidate. The Democrats, however, failed to unite behind a single candidate; their convention in Charleston, South Carolina, broke up after a bitter debate between Northern and Southern Democrats over slavery.

Lincoln on Slavery

Abraham Lincoln, the Republican Party's candidate, had had only a modestly influential political career, but he was, in 1860, a well-known politician. He had served in the Illinois state legislature and, later, in the House of Representatives for a single term. In 1858, Lincoln had gained a national reputation for his unsuccessful race for the U.S. Senate against Stephen Douglas. During that Senate campaign, Lincoln and Douglas had engaged in a series of debates, mainly on the issue of slavery, that received national attention. The full texts of the Lincoln-Douglas debates had been printed in newspapers around the country.

In 1860 Lincoln did not consider himself an abolitionist, but early in his life he had formed a distaste for slavery. He had been born into a family of very modest means—his parents were illiterate—and he had, through hard work, turned himself into a successful lawyer and politician. Lincoln believed that all Americans, including African

Americans, should have the ability to do with their lives what he had done with his. Slaves, however, did not have the opportunity to become educated or to improve their stations in life; most slaves remained in bondage their entire lives.

But Lincoln did not favor the immediate abolition of slavery. He believed that slavery was protected by the U.S. Constitution, and as president he would promise to uphold the Constitution. But Lincoln opposed the spread of slavery into new states or territories; he maintained that America's founding fathers, the men who had drafted the Con-

Although Lincoln opposed the spread of slavery to new states or territories, he believed that the rights of existing slaveholders were protected by the Constitution.

stitution, desired to allow slavery only in the places in which it already existed, not in new territories. Lincoln hoped that slavery would eventually die out in the South. Like many other antislavery Americans in 1860, Lincoln also argued that African Americans, once freed from slavery, should have the right to leave the United States and migrate to a new homeland in Africa.

Lincoln Wins the White House

During the presidential campaign of 1860, Northern Democratic candidate Stephen Douglas tried to depict Lincoln as an extremist on the issue of slavery whose election would prompt Southern states to secede from the Union and lead the nation into civil war. Lincoln refuted Douglas by articulating what he called a "middle ground" on slavery: As president, he would defend slavery in the areas in which it already existed but would oppose any extension of slavery into new states and territories.

On election day Lincoln's opposition fragmented, and he carried the election. Lincoln won only 40 percent of the popular vote, but he carried 180 electoral votes to 72 for Southern Democratic candidate

John Breckinridge, 39 for Whig canidate John Bell, and only 12 for Douglas. Lincoln won the electoral votes of all the Northern states, and the Southern states divided their votes among Lincoln's three opponents. In March 1861 Lincoln would become the nation's sixteenth president.

The South Secedes from the Union

Soon after the election of 1860, Douglas's prediction about the disintegration of the Union came true. In December the South Carolina legislature,

Stephen Douglas, a Northern Democratic candidate in the 1860 election, tried to depict Lincoln as an antislavery extremist.

reacting to Lincoln's election, voted 169–0 to withdraw from the United States. In January Mississippi followed South Carolina's lead, as did Florida, Alabama, Georgia, Louisiana, and, in February, Texas. Representatives from the seceded states met in Montgomery, Alabama, and formed the Confederate States of America, with Jefferson Davis as president. Most of the South was now in open rebellion against the Lincoln presidency, even though he had not yet taken office. Only four slave states—Maryland, Delaware, Kentucky, and Missouri—would ultimately remain loyal to the Union.

Lincoln maintained that the Union was a permanent entity, that no individual state could withdraw from it. He considered secession an act of rebellion that must be dealt with immediately. But Lincoln was not yet in office. President James Buchanan spoke against the South's secession; but as a lame-duck president in office for only a few more months, Buchanan could do little to prompt the rebellious Southern states to return to the Union.

When Lincoln took office on March 4, 1861, he tried, in his first inaugural address, to reach out to the rebellious South to avoid a costly and inevitable civil war. He promised that he had no intention of trying to abolish slavery in the states where it already existed: "I have no purpose, directly or indirectly, to interfere with the institution of slavery in the States where it exists. I believe I have no lawful right to do so, and I have no inclination to do so." He also reminded the rebellious South that "the Union of these States is perpetual" and that any attempt by any state to leave the Union was "legally void." Moreover, Lincoln asserted that "the central idea of secession, is the essence of anarchy." Lincoln concluded his long address with poetic and conciliatory words of friendship:

> I am loath to close. We are not enemies, but friends. We must not be enemies. Though passion may have strained, it must not break our bonds of affection. The mystic chords of memory, stretching from every battle-field, and every patriot grave, to every living heart and hearthstone, all over this broad land, will yet swell the chorus of Union, when again touched, as surely they will be, by the better angels of our nature.[44]

The Coming of War

But the war came. It began in a crisis over Fort Sumter, a federal garrison situated in the harbor of Charleston, South Carolina. After withdrawing from the Union, South Carolina demanded the fort's evacuation. Lincoln refused; and on the morning of April 12, 1861, artillery batteries of the South Carolina militia opened fire on the lightly defended fort. After a day and a half of bombardment, the fort's commander, Major Robert Anderson, surrendered the garrison.

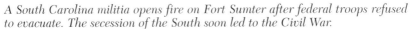

A South Carolina militia opens fire on Fort Sumter after federal troops refused to evacuate. The secession of the South soon led to the Civil War.

The South's act of secession had turned into civil war. The day after Fort Sumter's surrender, Lincoln called for the enlistment of seventy-five thousand troops to put down the Southern rebellion. Within weeks, Virginia, Arkansas, North Carolina, and Tennessee also withdrew from the Union and joined the Confederate States of America, giving the Confederacy eleven states.

The South's Early Victories

The North demanded swift retaliation for the Union's defeat at Fort Sumter. Northerners expected that the Southern rebellion could be put down swiftly by the well-trained federal army. But the North's first substantial attempt to defeat the Rebel army and arrest the rebellion ended in disaster. In July 1861, Brigadier General Irwin McDowell led a thirty-five-thousand-man army south from Washington, D.C., into Virginia. His target was a large Confederate army at the Manassas railroad junction. General McDowell reasoned that if he could smash that army, he could march unimpeded into the Confederate capital of Richmond, Virginia, and virtually end the rebellion.

Southern troops defeat McDowell's forces at the Battle of Bull Run. It became clear here that this war would have a higher death toll than expected.

But McDowell's forces were defeated by determined Rebel troops at Bull Run Creek, near Manassas, and the Yankees retreated to Washington, D.C. Casualties in the Battle of Bull Run had been much higher than anticipated—thirty-five hundred on both sides—making the North realize that the rebellion would not be suppressed in a few months. It would be a long and bloody war.

For the next two years, the South's armies were able to defend Southern soil. In crucial battles—at Bull Run again in August 1862, at Fredericksburg in December 1862, and at Chancellorsville in April 1863—the South's armies, under the brilliant leadership of General Robert E. Lee, soundly defeated Union armies. Until the spring of 1863, the South was winning the war.

A War over Secession

Although abolitionists like Harriet Beecher Stowe saw the Civil War, from the start, as a war to end slavery, for President Lincoln the conflict had begun as a battle over secession. His initial aim, when the war broke out, was to bring the rebellious Southern states back into the Union. Lincoln had no intention of making the abolition of slavery one of his war aims. For the first year of the war, Lincoln let it be known that the rebellious states could reenter the Union with the institution of slavery still intact.

As the war entered its second year, however, abolitionists in Congress began pressing Lincoln to take the bold step of freeing the slaves. Freeing the slaves might damage the South's ability to wage war because the labor performed by slaves would have to be performed by men who might otherwise enlist in the Confederate army.

Senator Charles Sumner of Massachusetts, a determined abolitionist, offered Lincoln another reason for freeing the slaves. Great Britain was considering recognizing the Confederacy as an independent nation and perhaps supporting the South's effort to free itself from the Union. England had been siding with the South because British textile mills were heavily dependent on the South's cotton. Since the start of the war, the amount of cotton exported to Great Britain had significantly decreased, mainly because Lincoln had ordered a naval blockade of the South, preventing its merchant ships from sailing overseas. Sumner tried to convince Lincoln that if America's civil war became a war over slavery rather than a conflict over secession, the British would not recognize or aid the South. *Uncle Tom's Cabin* had been a runaway best-seller in Great Britain; the English public would not support the South in a war to save slavery.

Abraham Lincoln signs the Emancipation Proclamation. Lincoln's action allowed slaves to join the military and have freedom in the North.

Lincoln Acts

By the summer of 1862, Lincoln began to believe that freeing the slaves might be a necessary wartime measure. On September 22, 1862, five days after a determined performance by the Union army at the Battle of Antietam, Lincoln issued the Preliminary Emancipation Proclamation. That document announced that, as of January 1, 1863, slaves held in the states in rebellion against the Union "shall be then, thenceforward, and forever free,"[45] and the U.S. government and its military would defend that freedom. This proclamation warned the South that states in rebellion against the Union would lose their legal right to hold slaves after January 1, 1863. In that same document, Lincoln offered to put forward a plan that would allow slave owners in states loyal to the Union to give up their slaves and receive financial compensation from the federal government.

Lincoln hoped that this Preliminary Emancipation Proclamation might induce some Southern states to rejoin the Union and end their involvement with the war. But no state accepted Lincoln's offer. So on January 1, 1863, Lincoln issued his Emancipation Proclamation. That document clearly identified the emancipation of the slaves as "a fit and necessary war measure for suppressing said rebellion."[46] In other words, Lincoln was not freeing the slaves for moral or philosophical reasons; he was freeing the slaves as a necessary act of war, to deprive the rebellious South of one of its key assets.

The War to End Slavery

When Lincoln freed the slaves in the rebellious states, the purpose of the war changed. It was no longer a war to force the Rebels back into the Union; it was a war to end slavery. If the South won the war, the Confederate States of America would become an independent nation and slavery would remain in place throughout the South. If the North emerged victorious, the South would be forced back into the Union, and slavery would be forever outlawed.

Not all Northerners embraced this new war aim. Northern Democrats criticized Lincoln's proclamation, claiming that the nation would not support a war whose goal was to abolish slavery. Some Northern troops deserted; they refused to fight in a war to free the slaves. But Lincoln stayed his course. In 1858, in his famous "House Divided" speech, he had predicted that the United States could not remain as a nation half slave and half free: "A house divided against itself cannot stand."[47] After almost two years of war, Lincoln had realized that reuniting his divided house would be impossible unless slavery were eliminated.

The Battle of Gettysburg

Lincoln's Emancipation Proclamation had little immediate effect because the South was winning the war. In the summer of 1863, however, the tide of the war changed in a great battle in the small town of Gettysburg, Pennsylvania.

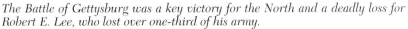

The Battle of Gettysburg was a key victory for the North and a deadly loss for Robert E. Lee, who lost over one-third of his army.

General Robert E. Lee, confident because of his recent battlefield victories over Northern troops, decided on a bold plan to end the war. He would invade the North, capture one or two key Northern cities, and force Lincoln to the peace table. In late June 1863, Lee began moving northward with his army of 73,000 men into Maryland and then into southern Pennsylvania. A large Union army of 110,000 men moved northward from Washington, D.C., with Lee.

On July 1 the two great armies met and clashed in the town of Gettysburg. For two days the battle raged with neither side claiming an advantage. On the third day, in a risky military maneuver, Lee sent thirteen thousand men under the command of Major General George Pickett into the center of the Union line, an attempt to puncture the federal defenses and rout the Union army. But Pickett's men were cut to pieces by Union cannon and rifle fire. Of the thirteen thousand Rebel soldiers involved in "Pickett's Charge," seven thousand were killed, wounded, or captured. Sensing defeat, Lee retreated to Virginia.

The Battle of Gettysburg was the turning point of the war. Lee had suffered his first major defeat, and he had lost more than one-third of his army. At the same time, a Northern army under the command of General Ulysses S. Grant had captured the key city of Vicksburg, Mississippi, on the Mississippi River. The Union now held the advantage in the war.

Lincoln at Gettysburg

Four months after the Battle of Gettysburg, in November 1863, President Lincoln traveled to that town to participate in a ceremony dedicating a national cemetery for those who lost their lives in the great battle that took place there. Lincoln was not the ceremony's keynote speaker; that honor went to Edward Everett, a nationally known orator. Lincoln was asked to offer a few appropriate words after Everett's speech, which lasted two hours.

In his Gettysburg Address, Lincoln articulated the war's meaning for those present at the ceremony and for other Americans who would read his speech in newspapers. He began by reminding his audience that America's founding fathers had established "a new nation, conceived in liberty and dedicated to the proposition that all men are created equal." He explained that this proposition was now being tested by this great civil war; he noted the purpose of the day's ceremony—to dedicate "a final resting place for those who here gave their lives that that nation might live." Then Lincoln went on to examine his purpose "in a larger sense." He urged his audience to continue the work begun by those who had fallen at Gettysburg. He concluded by asserting that those killed at Gettysburg "shall not have died in vain" because their nation "shall have a new birth of freedom."[48]

Abraham Lincoln delivers the Gettysburg Address.

Lincoln never used the words *slave* or *slavery* in his Gettysburg address; he did not speak specifically of racial inequalities. But he clearly informed Americans of the meaning of their terrible civil war. It was not a war over the Union; it was a war about equality, a war that would determine whether every American, regardless of race, would have equal opportunity to work, to earn and save money, to live in peace, to be free. It was a war fought to determine whether the 4 million Uncle Toms and Aunt Chloes held as slaves would remain in bondage forever or would be granted the rights and privileges that white Americans often took for granted.

The North's Victory

The tide of the war clearly changed after the North's victory at Gettysburg. Lee's troops fought on stubbornly for almost two more years; but by the winter of 1865, a Union victory seemed inevitable. Sensing victory close at hand, Lincoln once again identified the purpose of this terrible civil war in his second inaugural address, delivered on March 4, 1865:

One eighth of the whole population [of the United States] were colored slaves. . . . These slaves constituted a peculiar and powerful interest. All knew that this interest was, somehow, the cause of the war. To strengthen, perpetuate, and extend this interest was the object for which the insurgents would rend the Union, even by war; while the government claimed no right to do more than to restrict the territorial enlargement of it.[49]

In his address, Lincoln goes on to identify slavery as a terrible offense that God punished by sending to the North and the South "this terrible war, as the woe due to those by whom the offense came."[50]

One month later, the war ended as General Robert E. Lee surrendered the last large Rebel army. Yet Lincoln did not live to see his nation reunited. On April 14, 1865, Lincoln, while enjoying a theater performance with his wife, was shot in the head by John Wilkes Booth, a bitter Southerner who blamed Lincoln for the South's defeat. Lincoln died the next morning.

The Thirteenth Amendment

Before his death, Lincoln had become concerned that his Emancipation Proclamation would not permanently free all American slaves. Indeed, that measure did not free the slaves in the four slave states that had remained loyal to the Union—Missouri, Delaware, Kentucky, and Maryland. Furthermore, Lincoln foresaw the possibility of the U.S. Supreme Court ruling his Emancipation Proclamation unconstitutional. The only way to prohibit slavery forever was to pass a constitutional amendment that would outlaw slavery throughout the nation.

In April 1864, a year before the conclusion of the Civil War, the Thirteenth Amendment to the Constitution, an amendment abolishing slavery, was proposed in the U.S. Senate. The amendment would have to be passed by two-thirds of the Senate, two-thirds of the House of Representatives, and three-fourths of the state legislatures to become part of the Constitution. The amendment passed the Senate quickly, but it was not adopted by the House of Representatives until January 1865. And not until September 18, 1865, eight months after Lincoln's death, did the Thirteenth Amendment receive the approval of three-fourths of the state legislatures to become a permanent part of the Constitution.

The Thirteenth Amendment consists of two sections, each only one sentence long:

Section 1. Neither slavery nor involuntary servitude, except as a punishment for crime whereof the party shall have been duly convicted, shall exist within the United States, or any place subject to their jurisdiction.

Section 2. Congress shall have the power to enforce this article by appropriate legislation.

Free at Last

The Thirteenth Amendment officially abolished slavery in America. For almost 250 years, slavery had existed on American soil. It was certainly not a single novel by Harriet Beecher Stowe that had eradicated slavery from the United States. An active American abolitionist movement commenced two decades before Stowe picked up her pen to write the story of Uncle Tom. Ten years after the publication of *Uncle Tom's Cabin*, a bloody civil war was fought to determine whether slavery would continue to exist in the South. And finally, after that war, lawmakers had to amend the U.S. Constitution to ensure that slavery would never again resurface in America.

Members of the House of Representatives celebrate after passing the Thirteenth Amendment, which legally banished slavery in America.

Nonetheless, Lincoln's assertion that Stowe's novel had ignited the Civil War is not a complete exaggeration. The publication of *Uncle Tom's Cabin* fueled the controversy over slavery that occupied the United States during the 1850s. In the face of Stowe's critique, Southerners defended slavery more vehemently while Northerners attacked the institution more passionately. That polarization led to the great civil war that resulted in the elimination of slavery from the United States forever.

CHAPTER 5 The Legacy of Uncle Tom's Cabin

Uncle Tom's Cabin has become one of the most controversial novels in American literary history. Harriet Beecher Stowe's book was, of course, controversial when it first appeared in 1852. The novel received strong support from Northern reviewers and readers, and it was condemned as abolitionist trash by Southerners. During the next century and a half, American literary critics and literary historians have taken equally strong positions on the novel, some calling it one of the most influential works in American literary history and others claiming that it is a dated book without appeal for contemporary readers or, worse, a text that perpetuates negative racial stereotypes.

Uncle Tom's Cabin After the Civil War

Although the Civil War permanently settled the issue of slavery in the United States, *Uncle Tom's Cabin* remained popular in the North during the postwar decades. In 1899 Stowe's antislavery novel was still checked out more often than any other book in the New York Public Library.

Stowe's fiction published after *Uncle Tom's Cabin* also earned generally good reviews and enjoyed solid sales, though none of her later novels ever received the same attention as *Uncle Tom's Cabin*. In her novels after *Uncle Tom's Cabin* and *Dred: A Tale of the Great Dismal Swamp* (1856)—*The Minister's Wooing*, (1859), *The Pearl of Orr's Island* (1862), *Oldtown Folks* (1869), *My Wife and I* (1871), *Palmetto Leaves* (1873), *Pogonuc People* (1878)—Stowe turned her attention away from racial and political issues and focused mainly on New England life. But many readers who had been moved by *Uncle Tom's Cabin* followed Stowe's literary

The front page of Harper's Weekly, *featuring* Uncle Tom's Cabin.

Uncle Tom's Cabin on Stage

Soon after the success of *Uncle Tom's Cabin* became apparent, professional singer Asa Hutchinson asked for Harriet Beecher Stowe's permission to adapt the novel for the stage. Stowe, like many traditional Christians of the nineteenth century, however, opposed theatrical entertainment and refused. A short time later playwright George L. Aiken made the same request, and Stowe approved. Aiken eventually wrote three versions of *Uncle Tom's Cabin* for the stage. The first comprised only the first two-thirds of the novel, from the opening scene to the death of Eva St. Clare. The second version dealt with the last third of the novel. The third version, a long play consisting of six acts and thirty scenes, combined elements of the first two versions. This complete version of the play *Uncle Tom's Cabin* first appeared on stage in Troy, New York, on November 15, 1852. The play received rave reviews and ran for more than fifty performances. The following summer the play opened at the National Theatre in New York City, where it enjoyed a long and successful run. The play also succeeded in integrating the American theater. Before *Uncle Tom's Cabin* hit the stage, American theaters banned African Americans from attending performances. When the play opened at the National Theatre, however, the theater's management allowed African Americans to see the show, though they were restricted to certain seating areas.

The play version of *Uncle Tom's Cabin* eventually traveled around the Northern states, and many more people saw it than actually read Stowe's novel. The play was also exported to both Great Britain and France, where it enjoyed good reviews and large audiences.

Even after the Civil War, the stage version of *Uncle Tom's Cabin* remained popular in American theaters. The text of the play, however, was changed many times during the next hundred years. For example, a 1975 version of the play, performed by the Workshop of the Players' Art in the Bowery in New York City, featured black characters who were more rebellious than those in Stowe's novel and in Aiken's version of the play. A stage adaptation of *Uncle Tom's Cabin* that ran at Trinity Square Repertory Company in Providence, Rhode Island, had Uncle Tom, in a fantasy scene, shoot Augustine St. Clare.

During the past fifty years, stage versions of *Uncle Tom's Cabin* have been performed in Russia, China, and several European countries.

career by buying or reading her later novels.

Literary critics and historians of the late nineteenth century also noted the important place that *Uncle Tom's Cabin* held in American literary history. Writing around the turn of the nineteenth century, the novelist and critic Henry James remembered the great impact that Stowe's novel had on himself and the nation. Another noted novelist and critic, William Dean Howells, called *Uncle Tom's Cabin* "the great American novel"[51] in an

Author Mark Twain praised Stowe's antislavery novel.

essay that he wrote in 1898. Mark Twain, author of *Adventures of Huckleberry Finn*, also praised Stowe's great antislavery novel.

Some turn-of-the-century literary historians maintained that Stowe's novel contained artistic flaws. For example, in *A Literary History of America*, published in 1900, Barrett Wendell, a professor of English literature at Harvard University, stated that *Uncle Tom's Cabin* had been "written carelessly" and that it contained a "conventional and rambling" plot. Nonetheless, Wendell praised the novel as a "remarkable piece of fiction"[52] despite these flaws.

In the South during the postwar years, *Uncle Tom's Cabin* continued to receive severe criticism. Some Southern critics and historians continued to hold Stowe partly responsible for the South's defeat in the Civil War and for the South's economic problems during the post war years as the region coped with the loss of slave labor. Typical of this view was a comment written in a 1932 autobiography by the Louisiana writer Grace King, who had seen Stowe during an 1888 visit to Hartford, where Stowe spent her final years. "Harriet Beecher Stowe!" wrote King. "She . . . had brought the war upon us, as I had been taught, and all our misfortunes!"[53]

Uncle Tom's Cabin in the Twentieth Century

As the slavery era receded into the American past, *Uncle Tom's Cabin* began to lose both its readership and its place of importance in the American literary canon. After World War I, an important

Harriet Beecher Stowe, 1811–1896

Harriet Beecher Stowe was not yet forty years old when she began writing *Uncle Tom's Cabin*. The novel made her an instant celebrity. She toured the United States and Europe as the most famous author of her day. In England, she met Charles Dickens and other important members of the London literary establishment. She was welcomed in the courts of Europe as the American woman who wrote the great novel on American slavery.

Stowe's literary career did not end with *Uncle Tom's Cabin*. She wrote several more novels, a book of stories, and, with her sister, Catharine Beecher, *The American Woman's Home*, a guide to establishing and maintaining a household written for American homemakers, as well as several other books.

Stowe and her husband, Calvin, spent their retirement years in Hartford, Connecticut, in a home that is now preserved by the Stowe-Day Foundation and is open to visitors. The Stowes' next-door neighbor was Mark Twain, the great American humorist and novelist. Calvin Stowe died in 1886; Harriet died ten years later. Her first biographer was her son Charles Edward, who authored *Life of Harriet Beecher Stowe Compiled from Her Letters and Journals*, published in 1889.

Harriet Beecher Stowe

group of young writers arrived on the American literary scene. These writers—Ernest Hemingway, F. Scott Fitzgerald, John Dos Passos—became known as the Lost Generation, and they wrote about a world torn apart during and after the Great War. To the literary critics and historians who tuned into the message of the writers of the Lost Generation, *Uncle Tom's Cabin* seemed to be a badly dated book, a sentimental novel about a time in America's distant past that had lost its relevance in the wake of World War I.

Representative of this response to Stowe's antislavery masterpiece was a comment by Vernon L. Parrington in his book *Main Currents in American Thought*, published in 1927. Parrington called *Uncle Tom's Cabin* "noble propaganda"[54] rather than a great work of art. In other words, Parrington believed that Stowe's novel was effective in rallying the nation against slavery, but the book lacked artistic merit. Many twentieth-century literary critics also judged *Uncle Tom's Cabin* as excessively sentimental and melodramatic—a novel that appealed mainly to the emotions of mid–nineteenth-century readers, often provoking tears. According to these critics, once slavery had disappeared from the American landscape, the emotional appeal of Stowe's novel sharply decreased.

By the middle of the twentieth century, *Uncle Tom's Cabin* had lost its position among the American classics. It was not frequently assigned in college literature courses, and Stowe was only rarely the subject of articles in scholarly journals or academic conferences. Alfred Kazin, a twentieth-century American literary historian, points out that *Uncle Tom's Cabin* "was virtually out of print in the middle of the twentieth century."[55]

Frederick Douglass criticized Stowe's suggestion that freed slaves should start their own colony in Africa.

The African American Response

Uncle Tom's Cabin has received both enthusiastic praise and serious criticism from African American literary scholars. When the novel was first published, most African Americans, particularly those involved in the abolitionist movement, applauded the book as an honest depiction of the evils of American slavery. Frederick Douglass admired

Anti–Uncle Tom Novels

Between 1852 and the beginning
of the Civil War, Southern authors
produced more than a dozen novels
that attempted to respond to *Uncle Tom's
Cabin*. These novels, which became known as
anti–Uncle Tom novels, generally feature a kindly
slave owner—who treats his slaves with love and respect—and dutiful slaves—who prefer to live their lives in
bondage to a life of freedom. The slaves are completely loyal to
their masters and swoon in sadness when some illness or death
visits the master's house. When slaves misbehave, their punishment is generally mild. If a severe punishment like a whipping
occurs, it is only because a slave has committed a serious offense; and after his punishment, the slave pledges to reform
himself and forever end his bad ways. Sometimes a slave featured in an anti–Uncle Tom novel runs away from the plantation,
and he yearns to return.

Examples of anti–Uncle Tom novels include Mary Eastman's *Aunt
Phillis's Cabin; or Southern Life as It Is*, published in 1856; John Page's
*Uncle Robin and His Cabin in Virginia, and Tom Without One in
Boston* (1853); and Martha Haines Butt's *Antifanaticism: A Tale of the
South* (1853). These novels sold well, particularly in the South, during
the decade before the Civil War.

the novel, but he did criticize Stowe's suggestion toward the end of
the book that African Americans, once freed from slavery, should
find their own homeland in Africa. Writing to Stowe about freed
slaves removing to Africa, Douglass stated, "The truth is, dear
madame, we are *here*, and here we are likely to remain."[56] Douglass
was not alone in his criticism of Stowe's plan to create a colony in
Africa for free African Americans. In 1853 African American delegates to the Foreign Anti-Slavery Society's annual convention
passed a resolution condemning Stowe's colonization views.

Some African American critics of the mid–nineteenth century also
found fault with Stowe's portrayal of Uncle Tom. They found the
character to be too submissive. These critics wished that Uncle Tom
had been more like George Harris, had tried to escape from slavery,
had resisted Simon Legree more forcefully, or had acted on the slave
woman Cassy's suggestion that he kill Simon Legree, to which Tom
replies, "No! good never comes of wickedness. . . . The dear, blessed
Lord never shed no blood but his own, and that he poured out for

us when we was enemies. Lord, help us to follow his steps, and love our enemies."[57] In the twentieth century, the term *Uncle Tom* became an insult. An individual described as an Uncle Tom is a black person who is too timid and submissive to demand and agitate for his civil rights.

But Stowe has always had African American defenders as well. Booker T. Washington, writing just after the turn of the twentieth century, asserted that Stowe "so stirred the hearts of the Northern people that a large part of them were ready either to vote, or, in the last extremity, to fight for the suppression of slavery. The value of *Uncle Tom's Cabin* to the cause of Abolition can never be justly estimated."[58] In 1898 Paul Lawrence Dunbar, an African American poet and novelist, published a poem titled "Harriet Beecher Stowe," which opened with these lines:

> She told the story and the whole world wept
> At wrongs and cruelties it had not known
> But for this fearless woman's voice alone
> She spoke to consciences that long had slept;[59]

James Baldwin's Critique

In 1949 James Baldwin, who would become known as one of the most important African American essayists and novelists of the twentieth century, published an essay on *Uncle Tom's Cabin* that would greatly influence the way African American readers would view Stowe's novel. In his essay, titled "Everybody's Protest Novel," Baldwin, who as a boy read *Uncle Tom's Cabin* "over and over and over again,"[60] calls Stowe's novel "a very bad novel."[61] In Baldwin's view, Stowe's novel is excessively sentimental and reads like a political pamphlet, not like a novel.

Baldwin also criticizes Stowe's black characters. He dismisses George and Eliza Harris, asserting that they are not really African Americans because they are so light

James Baldwin criticized Stowe's novel for what he saw as inaccurate portrayals of African Americans.

Uncle Tom's Cabin Abroad

Uncle Tom's Cabin has always enjoyed solid sales outside the United
States. Immediately after the novel's
publication in book form, it was exported to
Great Britain, where it sold in great numbers.
Most British citizens were appalled that slavery remained legal in the United States, and they identified with
Harriet Beecher Stowe's powerful antislavery message. When
Stowe visited Great Britain in the Spring of 1853, she was already
a literary celebrity. Literate British citizens from all walks of life had
read *Uncle Tom's Cabin.*

Eventually, *Uncle Tom's Cabin* would become a popular novel in
other nations as well. Stowe's book has been translated into more than
a dozen languages. Young students and professional scholars around
the world read and discuss *Uncle Tom's Cabin* for both its literary
value and its ability to capture the era of slavery in the United States.

During the twentieth century, Stowe's novel enjoyed a particularly
respectful reception in the former Soviet Union. Just as American students read Aleksandr Solzhenitsyn's *The Gulag Archipelago* and other
texts highlighting the worst atrocities of the Soviet system of government, Russian students read *Uncle Tom's Cabin.* Many Russian readers view Stowe's novel as evidence of the evils of American capitalist
economic system, which allowed the buying and selling of human beings for financial profit.

Uncle Tom's Cabin remains one of the most commonly read American novels abroad. Around the world, Stowe's masterpiece has found
a place in bookstores, libraries, and classrooms.

skinned that they could pass as whites. Baldwin condemns Stowe for
making her novel's hero, Uncle Tom, illiterate and humble, concerned
only about his relationship with God. According to Baldwin, Uncle
Tom "has been robbed of his humanity and divested of his sex."[62]

Baldwin's "Everybody's Protest Novel" would influence the way
African American scholars and readers viewed *Uncle Tom's Cabin* during the 1950s and 1960s, the time of the civil rights movement. During
these decades, African Americans actively protested for their civil
rights, demanding an end to racial segregation and discrimination in
the United States. These protests often took the form of public
marches and demonstrations. For African Americans involved in the
civil rights movement, the passive and humble Uncle Tom became a
poor role model.

Ardent Defenders

In the face of the attack on *Uncle Tom's Cabin* waged by James Baldwin, several noteworthy American literary critics came to Stowe's defense. In 1948 Edmund Wilson, a prominent literary historian, defended Stowe's masterwork in *Patriotic Gore*, his study of the literature of the Civil War era. Wilson called *Uncle Tom's Cabin* "a much more remarkable book than one had ever been allowed to suspect" with characters who "spring to life with . . . vitality."[63] Similarly, in 1957, Lionel Trilling, another prominent post–World War II American literary critic, wrote that "no other single book has ever so directly influenced the course of history" and that "no other work has contributed so many legendary figures to American life."[64]

American literary critic Edmund Wilson defended Uncle Tom's Cabin, *calling it a "remarkable" book.*

Some American critics of the 1960s tried to defend Stowe's novel by making comparisons between Uncle Tom and Martin Luther King Jr., who consistently advocated nonviolent resistance as a tactic to agitate for civil rights. Critics of King's passive approach, however, often accused the civil rights leader of being an Uncle Tom.

Rediscovered by Feminists

During the 1960s *Uncle Tom's Cabin* was rediscovered by American feminist literary critics and historians. Since that time, feminist critics and historians have looked back to the eighteenth and nineteenth centuries to rediscover the works of American female writers that have been forgotten or have fallen out of favor. Feminist critics such as Elizabeth Ammons, Jean Fagan Yellin, Ann Douglas, and Jane Tompkins have become the novel's most ardent defenders.

Ann Douglas applauds Stowe for daring to speak out against slavery and attempting to influence the political will of the American people. During Stowe's time, women were pressured to stay out of the political arena; but slavery was an institution that damaged women in unique ways—by separating children from their mothers and by allowing slave women to be sexually exploited by their masters—and Stowe addressed these concerns in her novel. As Jean Fagan Yellin has asserted, "*Uncle Tom's Cabin*, written three years after the meeting at Seneca Falls where feminists had spelled out their demands for full participation in American life, dramatizes women's roles in the fight against chattel slavery in America."[65]

These critics have found in Stowe's novel a powerful feminist message. In a 1978 essay, Jane Tompkins argued that Stowe's *Uncle Tom's Cabin* was the best of a body of mid–nineteenth-century novels by American female writers that attempt to give women "the central position of power and authority in the culture."[66] In *Uncle Tom's Cabin*, according to Tompkins, Stowe puts forth a plan to reorganize America's moral culture based on the values of motherly love and Christian redemption. Elizabeth Ammons applauds Stowe for paving the way for other important female writers of the nineteenth century such as Louisa May Alcott, Harriet Wilson, Frances Ellen Harper, and Sarah Orne Jewett.

The current interest in *Uncle Tom's Cabin* by feminist literary scholars suggests that Stowe's novel is not outdated; it continues to move today's students of American fiction who wish to learn more about the institution of slavery, the religious beliefs of the nineteenth century, the lives of nineteenth-century women, and the political ideas of Stowe's day. Few literary historians would discount the enormous impact that *Uncle Tom's Cabin* had on America when it first appeared. Stowe's novel, however, did not cease to be of interest to readers when the Civil War abolished slavery. *Uncle Tom's Cabin* will probably continue to captivate readers throughout the twenty-first century as well.

Appendix

Excerpts from Original Documents Pertaining to *Uncle Tom's Cabin*.

Document 1: A Slave Auction Advertisement

This advertisement, placed in a Jackson, Tennessee, newspaper in 1860, announces the auction of land and negroes. During such a sale, land and slave families would be split apart.

In Madison Co. Court!
LARGE SALE OF
LAND AND NEGROES

Petition for Sale of Land and Slaves.

Albert G. McClellan and others

vs.

Mary Vaden and husband, G. W. Vaden and others, distributees of Isabella McClellan, dec'd.

In the above cause, the undersigned, Clerk of the County Court of Madison county, Tenn., as commissioner, will expose to public sale on Saturday, 24th of March next, at the Court house, in the town of Jackson, that most desirable and conveniently situated Tract of Land, known as the McClellan farm, contianing

1000 ACRES.

in one body, and lying within a mile and a half of the town of Jackson. Also, at the same time and place,

18 Or 20 NEGROES,

consisting of men, women and children. The land will be divided into tracts previous to the day of sale, and each division will be sold seperately.

Terms of sale.—Land on a credit of one and two years, and the negroes upon a credit of 12 months from the day of sale. Notes, with good security, will be required of purchasers, and lien retained on both land and negroes for the purchase money. Title t. the land and negroes indisputable.

P. C. McCOWAT,

C. & M. Commissioner

Feb. 24, 1860.

$100 REWARD!

RANAWAY

From the undersigned, living on Current River, about twelve miles above Doniphan, in Ripley County, Mo., on 2nd of March, 1860, A NE GRO MAN, about 30 years old, weighs about 160 pounds; high forehead, with a scar on it; had on brown pants and coat very much worn, and an old black wool hat; shoes size No. 11.

The above reward will be given to any person who may apprehend this said negro out of the State; and fifty dollars if apprehended in this State outside of Ripley county, or $25 if taken in Ripley county.

APOS TUCKER.

Document 2: Advertisement for a Runaway Slave

This newspaper advertisement announces a reward for a runaway Missouri slave, unnamed, who bears a scar on his forehead. Many slaves escaped from slavery by crossing the Ohio River into the free state of Ohio, where Harriet Beecher Stowe lived for eighteen years.

Document 3: The Conversion of Senator Bird

Chapter 9 of Uncle Tom's Cabin *is set in the Ohio home of Senator and Mrs. Bird, who engage in a debate over the Fugitive Slave Law. Mrs. Bird convinces her husband that such a law is immoral. When Eliza Harris and her son arrive at the Bird's home, Mr. and Mrs. Bird break the law by assisting her. Some literary critics point out that Mrs. Bird, in attitude and appearance, resembles Harriet Beecher Stowe.*

The light of the cheerful fire shone on the rug and carpet of a cosey parlor, and glittered on the sides of the tea-cups and well-brightened teapot, as Senator Bird was drawing off his boots, preparatory to inserting his feet in a pair of new handsome slippers, which his wife had been working for him while away on his senatorial tour. Mrs. Bird, looking the very picture of delight, was superintending the arrangements of the table, ever and anon mingling admonitory remarks to a number of frolicsome juveniles, who were effervescing in all those modes of untold gambol and mischief that have astonished mothers ever since the flood.

"Tom, let the door-knob alone,—there's a man! Mary! Mary! don't pull the cat's tail,—poor pussy! Jim, you mustn't climb on that table,—no, no!—You don't know, my dear, what a surprise it is to us all, to see you here to-night!" said she, at last, when she found a space to say something to her husband.

"Yes, yes, I thought I'd just make a run down, spend the night,and have a little comfort at home. I'm tired to death, and my head aches!"

Mrs. Bird cast a glance at a camphor-bottle, which stood in the half open closet, and appeared to meditate an approach to it, but her husband interposed.

"No, no, Mary, no doctoring! a cup of your good hot tea, and some of our good home living, is what I want. It's a tiresome business, this legislating!"

And the senator smiled, as if he rather liked the idea of considering himself a sacrifice to his country.

"Well," said his wife, after the business of the tea table was getting rather slack, "and what have they been doing in the Senate?" Now, it was a very unusual thing for gentle little Mrs. Bird ever to trouble her head with what was going on in the house of the state, very wisely considering that she had enough to do to mind her own. Mr. Bird, therefore, opened his eyes in surprise, and said,

"Not very much of importance."

"Well; but is it true that they have been passing a law forbidding people to give meat and drink to those poor colored folks that come along? I heard they were talking of some such law, but I didn't think any Christian legislature would pass it!"

"Why, Mary, you are getting to be a politician, all at once."

"No, nonsense! I wouldn't give a fip for all your politics, generally, but I think this is something downright cruel and unchristian. I hope, my dear, no such law has been passed."

"There has been a law passed forbidding people to help off the slaves that come over from Kentucky, my dear; so much of that thing has been done by these reckless Abolitionists, that our brethren in Kentucky are very strongly excited, and it seems necessary, and no more than Christian and kind, that something should be done by our state to quiet the excitement."

"And what is the law? It don't forbid us to shelter those poor creatures a night, does it, and to give 'em something comfortable to eat, and a few old clothes, and send them quietly about their business?"

"Why, yes, my dear; that would be aiding and abetting, you know."

Mrs. Bird was a timid, blushing little woman, of about four feet in height, and with mild blue eyes, and a peach-blow complexion, and the gentlest, sweetest voice in the world;—as for courage, a moderate-sized cock-turkey had been known to put her to rout at the very first gobble, and a stout house-dog, of moderate capacity, would bring her into subjection merely by a show of his teeth. Her husband and children were her entire world, and in these she ruled more by entreaty and persuasion than by command or argument. There was only one thing that was capable of arousing her, and that provocation came in on the side of her unusually gentle and sympathetic nature;—anything in the shape of cruelty would throw her into a passion, which was the more alarming and inexplicable in proportion to the general softness of her nature. Generally the most indulgent and easy to be entreated of all mothers, still her boys had a very reverent remembrance of a most vehement chastisement she once bestowed on them, because she found them leagued with several graceless boys of the neighborhood, stoning a defenceless kitten.

"I'll tell you what," Master Bill used to say, "I was scared that time. Mother came at me so that I thought she was crazy, and I was whipped and tumbled off to bed, without any supper, before I could get over wondering what had come about; and, after that, I heard mother crying outside the door, which made me feel worse than all the rest. I'll tell you what," he'd say, "we boys never stoned another kitten!"

On the present occasion, Mrs. Bird rose quickly, with very red cheeks, which quite improved her general appearance, and walked up to her husband, with quite a resolute air, and said, in a determined tone,

"Now, John, I want to know if you think such a law as that is right and Christian?"

"You won't shoot me, now, Mary, if I say I do!"

"I never could have thought it of you, John; you didn't vote for it?"

"Even so, my fair politician."

"You ought to be ashamed, John! Poor, homeless, houseless creatures! It's a shameful, wicked, abominable law, and I'll break it, for one, the first time I get a chance; and I hope I *shall* have a chance, I do! Things have got to a pretty pass, if a woman can't give a warm supper and a bed to poor, starving creatures, just because they are slaves, and have been abused and oppressed all their lives, poor things!"

"But, Mary, just listen to me. Your feelings are all quite right, dear, and interesting, and I love you for them; but, then, dear, we mustn't suffer our feelings to run away with our judgment; you must consider it's a matter of private feeling,—there are great public interests involved,—there is such a state of public agitation rising, that we must put aside our private feelings."

"Now, John, I don't know anything about politics, but I can read my Bible; and there I see that I must feed the hungry, clothe the naked, and comfort the desolate; and that Bible I mean to follow."

"But in cases where your doing so would involve a great public evil—"

"Obeying God never brings on public evils. I know it can't. It's always safest, all round, to *do as He* bids us.

"Now, listen to me, Mary, and I can state to you a very clear argument, to show—"

"O, nonsense, John! you can talk all night, but you wouldn't do it. I put it to you, John,—would *you* now turn away a poor, shivering, hungry creature from your door, because he was a runaway? *Would* you, now?"

100

Now, if the truth must be told, our senator had the misfortune to be a man who had a particularly humane and accessible nature, and turning away anybody that was in trouble never had been his forte; and what was worse for him in this particular pinch of the argument was, that his wife knew it, and, of course was making an assault on rather an indefensible point. So he had recourse to the usual means of gaining time for such cases made and provided; he said "ahem," and coughed several times, took out his pocket-handkerchief, and began to wipe his glasses. Mrs. Bird, seeing the defenceless condition of the enemy's territory, had no more conscience than to push her advantage.

"I should like to see you doing that, John—I really should! Turning a woman out of doors in a snow storm, for instance; or may be you'd take her up and put her in jail, wouldn't you? You would make a great hand at that!"

"Of course, it would be a very painful duty," began Mr. Bird, in a moderate tone.

"Duty, John! don't use that word! You know it isn't a duty—it can't be a duty! If folks want to keep their slaves from running away, let 'em treat 'em well,—that's my doctrine. If I had slaves (as I hope I never shall have), I'd risk their wanting to run away from me, or you either, John. I tell you folks don't run away when they are happy; and when they do run, poor creatures! they suffer enough with cold and hunger and fear, without everybody's turning against them; and, law or no law, I never will, so help me God!"

"Mary! Mary! My dear, let me reason with you."

"I hate reasoning, John,—especially reasoning on such subjects. There's a way you political folks have of coming round and round a plain right thing; and you don't believe in it yourselves, when it comes to practice. I know *you* well enough, John. You don't be-lieve it's right any more than I do; and you wouldn't do it any sooner than I."

At this critical juncture, old Cudjoe, the black man-of-all-work, put his head in at the door, and wished "Missis would come into the kitchen;" and our senator, tolerably relieved, looked after his little wife with a whimsical mixture of amusement and vexation, and, seat-ing himself in the arm-chair, began to read the papers.

After a moment, his wife's voice was heard at the door, in a quick, earnest tone,—"John! John! I do wish you'd come here, a moment."

He laid down his paper, and went into the kitchen, and started, quite amazed at the sight that presented itself:—A young and slen-der woman, with garments torn and frozen, with one shoe gone, and the stocking torn away from the cut and bleeding foot, was laid back in a deadly swoon upon two chairs. There was the impress of the de-spised race on her face, yet none could help feeling its mournful and pathetic beauty, while its stony sharpness, its cold, fixed, deathly as-pect, struck a solemn chill over him. He drew his breath short, and stood in silence. His wife, and their only colored domestic, old Aunt Dinah, were busily engaged in restorative measures; while old Cudjoe had got the boy on his knee, and was busy pulling off his shoes and stockings, and chafing his little cold feet.

"Sure, now, if she an't a sight to behold!" said old Dinah, compassionately; "pears like 'twas the heat that made her faint. She was tol'able peart when she cum in, and asked if she couldn't warm herself here a spell; and I was just a askin' her where she cum from, and she fainted right down. Never done much hard work, guess, by the looks of her hands."

"Poor creature!" said Mrs. Bird, compassionately, as the woman slowly unclosed her large, dark eyes, and looked vacantly at her. Suddenly an expression of agony crossed her face, and she sprang up, saying, "O, my Harry! Have they got him?"

The boy, at this, jumped from Cudjoe's knee, and running to her side put up his arms. "O, he's here! he's here!" she exclaimed.

"O, ma'am!" said she, wildly, to Mrs. Bird, "do protect us! don't let them get him!"

"Nobody shall hurt you here, poor woman," said Mrs. Bird, encouragingly. "You are safe; don't be afraid."

"God bless you!" said the woman, covering her face and sobbing; while the little boy, seeing her crying, tried to get into her lap.

With many gentle and womanly offices, which none knew better how to render than Mrs. Bird, the poor woman was, in time, rendered more calm. A temporary bed was provided for her on the settle, near the fire; and, after a short time, she fell into a heavy slumber, with the child, who seemed no less weary, soundly sleeping on her arm; for the mother resisted, with nervous anxiety, the kindest attempts to take him from her; and, even in sleep, her arm encircled him with an unrelaxing clasp, as if she could not even then be beguiled of her vigilant hold.

Mr. and Mrs. Bird had gone back to the parlor, where, strange as it may appear, no reference was made, on either side, to the preceding conversation; but Mrs. Bird busied herself with her knitting work, and Mr. Bird pretended to be reading the paper.

"I wonder who and what she is!" said Mr. Bird, at last, as he laid it down.

"When she wakes up and feels a little rested, we will see," said Mrs. Bird.

"I say, wife!" said Mr. Bird after musing in silence over his newspaper.

"Well, dear!"

"She couldn't wear one of your gowns, could she, by any letting down, or such matter? She seems to be rather larger than you are."

A quite perceptible smile glimmered on Mrs. Bird's face, as she answered, "We'll see."

Another pause, and Mr. Bird again broke out,

"I say, wife!"

"Well! What now?"

"Why, there's that old bombazin cloak, that you keep on purpose to put over me when I take my afternoon's nap; you might as well give her that,—she needs clothes."

At this instant, Dinah looked in to say that the woman was awake, and wanted to see Missis.

Mr. and Mrs. Bird went into the kitchen, followed by the two eldest boys, the smaller fry having, by this time, been safely disposed of in bed.

The woman was now sitting up on the settle, by the fire. She was looking steadily into the blaze, with a calm, heartbroken expression, very different from her former agitated wildness.

"Did you want me?" said Mrs. Bird, in gentle tones. "I hope you feel better now, poor woman!"

A long drawn, shivering sigh was the only answer; but she lifted her dark eyes, and fixed them on her with such a forlorn and imploring expression, that the tears came into the little woman's eyes.

"You needn't be afraid of anything; we are friends here, poor woman! Tell me where you came from, and what you want," said she.

"I came from Kentucky," said the woman.

"When?" said Mr. Bird, taking up the interogatory.

"Tonight."

"How did you come?"

"I crossed on the ice."

"Crossed on the ice!" said every one present.

"Yes," said the woman, slowly, "I did. God helping me, I crossed on the ice; for they were behind me—right behind—and there was no other way!"

"Law, Missis," said Cudjoe, "the ice is all in broken-up blocks, a swinging and a tetering up and down in the water!"

"I know it was—I know it!" said she, wildly; "but I did it! I wouldn't have thought I could,—I didn't think I should get over, but I didn't care! I could but die, if I didn't. The Lord helped me; nobody knows how much the Lord can help 'em, till they try," said the woman, with a flashing eye.

"Were you a slave?" said Mr. Bird.

"Yes, sir; I belonged to a man in Kentucky."

"Was he unkind to you?"

"No, sir; he was a good master."

"And was your mistress unkind to you?"

"No, sir—no! my mistress was always good to me."

"What could induce you to leave a good home, then, and run away, and go through such dangers?"

The woman looked up at Mrs. Bird, with a keen, scrutinizing glance, and it did not escape her that she was dressed in deep mourning.

"Ma'am," she said, suddenly, "have you ever lost a child?"

The question was unexpected, and it was thrust on a new wound; for it was only a month since a darling child of the family had been laid in the grave.

Mr. Bird turned around and walked to the window, and Mrs. Bird burst into tears; but, recovering her voice, she said,

"Why do you ask that? I have lost a little one."

"Then you will feel for me. I have lost two, one after another,—left 'em buried there when I came away; and I had only this one left. I never slept a night without him; he was all I had. He was my comfort and pride, day and night; and, ma'am, they were going to take him away from me,—to *sell* him,—sell him down south, ma'am, to go all alone,—a baby that had never been away from his mother in his life! I couldn't stand it, ma'am. I knew I never should be good for anything, if they did; and when I knew the papers were signed, and he was sold, I took him and came off in the night; and they chased me,— the man that bought him, and some of Mas'r's folks,—and they were coming down right behind me, and I heard 'em. I jumped right on to the ice; and how I got across, I don't know,—but, first I knew, a man was helping me up the bank."

The woman did not sob nor weep. She had gone to a place where tears are dry; but every one around her was, in some way characteristic of themselves, showing signs of hearty sympathy.

The two little boys, after a desperate rummaging in their pockets, in search of those pocket-handkerchiefs which mothers know are never to be found there, had thrown themselves disconsolately into the skirts of their mother's gown, where they were sobbing, and wiping their eyes and noses, to their hearts' content;—Mrs. Bird had her face fairly hidden in her pocket-handkerchief; and old Dinah, with tears streaming down her black, honest face, was ejaculating, "Lord have mercy on us!" with all the fervor of a camp meeting;—while old Cudjoe, rubbing his eyes very hard with his cuffs, and making a most uncommon variety of wry faces, occasionally responded in the same key, with great fervor. Our senator was a statesman, and of course could not be expected to cry, like other mortals; and so he turned his back to the company, and looked out of the window, and seemed particularly busy in clearing his throat and wiping his spectacle glasses, occasionally blowing his nose in a manner that was calculated to excite suspicion, had any one been in a state to observe critically.

"How came you to tell me you had a kind master?" he suddenly exclaimed, gulping down very resolutely some kind of rising in his throat, and turning suddenly round upon the woman.

"Because he *was* a kind master; I'll say that of him, any way;—and my mistress was kind; but they couldn't help themselves. They were owing money; and there was some way, I can't tell how, that a man had a hold on them, and they were obliged to give him his will. I listened, and heard him telling mistress that, and she begging and pleading for me,—and he told her he couldn't help himself, and that the papers were all drawn;—and then it was I took him and left my home, and came away. I knew 't was no use of my trying to live, if they did it; for 't 'pears like this child is all I have."

"Have you no husband?"

"Yes, but he belongs to another man. His master is real hard to him, and won't let him come to see me, hardly ever; and he's grown harder and harder upon us, and he threatens to sell him down south;—it's like I'll never see *him* again!"

The quiet tone in which the woman pronounced these words might have led a superficial observer to think that she was entirely apathetic; but there was a calm, settled depth of anguish in her large, dark eyes, that spoke of something far otherwise.

"And where do you mean to go, my poor woman?" said Mrs. Bird.

"To Canada, if I only knew where that was. Is it very far off, is Canada?" said she, looking up, with a simple, confiding air, to Mrs. Bird's face.

"Poor thing!" said Mrs. Bird, involuntarily.

"Is 't a very great way off, think?" said the woman, earnestly.

"Much further than you think, poor child!" said Mrs. Bird; "but we will try to think what can be done for you. Here, Dinah, make her up a bed in your own room, close by the kitchen, and I'll think what to do for her in the morning. Meanwhile, never fear, poor woman; put your trust in God; he will protect you."

Mrs. Bird and her husband reentered the parlor. She sat down in her little rocking-chair before the fire, swaying thoughtfully to and fro. Mr. Bird strode up and down the room, grumbling to himself, "Pish! pshaw! confounded awkward business!" At length, striding up to his wife, he said,

"I say, wife, she'll have to get away from here, this very night. That fellow will be down on the scent bright and early tomorrow morning· if 't was only the woman, she could lie quiet till it was over; but that little chap can't be kept still by a troop of horse and foot, I'll warrant me; he'll bring it all out, popping his head out of some window or door. A pretty kettle of fish it would be for me, too, to be caught with them both here, just now! No; they'll have to be got off to-night."

"To-night! How is it possible?—where to?"

"Well, I know pretty well where to," said the senator, beginning to put on his boots, with a reflective air; and, stopping when his leg was half in, he embraced his knee with both hands, and seemed to go off in deep meditation.

"It's a confounded awkward, ugly business," said he, at last, beginning to tug at his boot-straps again, "and that's a fact!" After one boot was fairly on, the senator sat with the other in his hand, profoundly studying the figure of the carpet. "It will have to be done, though, for aught I see,—hang it all!" and he drew the other boot anxiously on, and looked out of the window.

Now, little Mrs. Bird was a discreet woman,—a woman who never in her life said, "I told you so!" and, on the present occasion, though pretty well aware of the shape her husband's meditations were taking, she very prudently forbore to meddle with them, only sat very quietly in her chair, and looked quite ready to hear her liege lord's intentions, when he should think proper to utter them.

"You see," he said, "there's my old client, Van Trompe, has come over from Kentucky, and set all his slaves free; and he has bought a place seven miles up the creek, here, back in the woods, where nobody goes, unless they go on purpose; and it's a place that isn't found in a hurry. There she'd be safe enough; but the plague of the thing is, nobody could drive a carriage there tonight, but *me*."

"Why not? Cudjoe is an excellent driver."

"Ay, ay, but here it is. The creek has to be crossed twice; and the second crossing is quite dangerous, unless one knows it as I do. I have crossed it a hundred times on horseback, and know exactly the turns to take. And so, you see, there's no help for it. Cudjoe must put in the horses, as quietly as may be, about twelve o'clock, and I'll take her over; and then, to give color to the matter, he must carry me on to the next tavern to take the stage for Columbus, that comes by about three or four, and so it will look as if I had had the carriage only for that. I shall get into business bright and early in the morning. But I'm thinking I shall feel rather cheap there, after all that's been said and done; but, hang it, I can't help it!"

"Your heart is better than your head, in this case, John," said the wife, laying her little white hand on his. "Could I ever have loved you, had I not known you better than you know yourself?" And the little woman looked so handsome, with the tears sparkling in her eyes, that the senator thought he must be a decidedly clever fellow, to get such a pretty creature into such a passionate admiration of him; and so, what could he do but walk off soberly, to see about the carriage. At the door, however, he stopped a moment, and then coming back, he said, with some hesitation.

"Mary, I don't know how you'd feel about it, but there's that drawer full of things—of—of—poor little Henry's." So saying, he turned quickly on his heel, and shut the door after him.

Document 4: The Death of Uncle Tom

Chapter 41 of Uncle Tom's Cabin *records the death of Uncle Tom. George Shelby, the son of Uncle Tom's original owner, arrives at the plantation of Simon Legree two days after Uncle Tom has received a brutal beating. George comes on the scene too late to save Uncle Tom's life, but he does hear Uncle Tom's final words: "Who,—who,—who shall separate us from the love of Christ?"*

106

Two days after, a young man drove a light wagon up through the avenue of China-trees, and, throwing the reins hastily on the horses' neck, sprang out and inquired for the owner of the place.

It was George Shelby; and, to show how he came to be there, we must go back in our story.

The letter of Miss Ophelia to Mrs. Shelby had, by some unfortunate accident, been detained, for a month or two, at some remote post-office, before it reached its destination; and, of course, before it was received, Tom was already lost to view among the distant swamps of the Red River.

Mrs. Shelby read the intelligence with the deepest concern; but any immediate action upon it was an impossibility. She was then in attendance on the sick-bed of her husband, who lay delirious in the crisis of a fever. Master George Shelby, who, in the interval, had changed from a boy to a tall young man, was her constant and faithful assistant, and her only reliance in superintending his father's affairs. Miss Ophelia had taken the precaution to send them the name of the lawyer who did business for the St. Clares; and the most that, in the emergency, could be done, was to address a letter of inquiry to him. The sudden death of Mr. Shelby, a few days after, brought, of course, an absorbing pressure of other interests, for a season.

Mr. Shelby showed his confidence in his wife's ability, by appointing her sole executrix upon his estates; and thus immediately a large and complicated amount of business was brought upon her hands.

Mrs. Shelby, with characteristic energy, applied herself to the work of straightening the entangled web of affairs; and she and George were for some time occupied with collecting and examining accounts, selling property and settling debts; for Mrs. Shelby was determined that everything should be brought into tangible and recognizable shape, let the consequences to her prove what they might. In the mean time, they received a letter from the lawyer to whom Miss Ophelia had referred them, saying that he knew nothing of the matter; that the man was sold at a public auction, and that, beyond receiving the money, he knew nothing of the affair.

Neither George nor Mrs. Shelby could be easy at this result; and, accordingly, some six months after, the latter, having business for his mother, down the river, resolved to visit New Orleans, in person, and push his inquiries, in hopes of discovering Tom's whereabouts, and restoring him.

After some months of unsuccessful search, by the merest accident, George fell in with a man, in New Orleans, who happened to be possessed of the desired information; and with his money in his pocket, our hero took steamboat for Red River, resolving to find out and repurchase his old friend.

He was soon introduced into the house, where he found Legree in the sitting-room.

Legree received the stranger with a kind of surly hospitality,

"I understand," said the young man, "that you bought, in New Orleans, a boy, named Tom. He used to be on my father's place, and I came to see if I couldn't buy him back."

Legree's brow grew dark, and he broke out, passionately: "Yes, I did buy such a fellow,—and a h—l of a bargain I had of it, too! The most rebellious, saucy, impudent dog! Set up my niggers to run away; got off two gals, worth eight hundred or a thousand dollars apiece. He owned to that, and, when I bid him tell me where they was, he up and said he knew, but he wouldn't tell; and stood to it, though I gave him the cussedest flogging I ever gave nigger yet. I b'lieve he's trying to die; but I don't know as he'll make it out."

"Where is he?" said George, impetuously. "Let me see him." The cheeks of the young man were crimson, and his eyes flashed fire; but he prudently said nothing, as yet.

"He's in dat ar shed," said a little fellow, who stood holding George's horse.

Legree kicked the boy, and swore at him; but George, without saying another word, turned and strode to the spot.

Tom had been lying two days since the fatal night; not suffering, for every nerve of suffering was blunted and destroyed. He lay, for the most part, in a quiet stupor; for the laws of a powerful and well-knit frame would not at once release the imprisoned spirit. By stealth, there had been there, in the darkness of the night, poor desolated creatures, who stole from their scanty hours' rest, that they might repay to him some of those ministrations of love in which he had always been so abundant. Truly, those poor disciples had little to give,—only the cup of cold water; but it was given with full hearts.

Tears had fallen on that honest, insensible face,—tears of late repentance in the poor, ignorant heathen, whom his dying love and patience had awakened to repentance, and bitter prayers, breathed over him to a late-found Saviour, of whom they scarce knew more than the name, but whom the yearning ignorant heart of man never implores in vain.

Cassy, who had glided out of her place of concealment, and, by overhearing, learned the sacrifice that had been made for her and Emmeline, had been there, the night before, defying the danger of detection; and, moved by the last few words which the affectionate soul had yet strength to breathe, the long winter of despair, the ice of years, had given way, and the dark, despairing woman had wept and prayed.

When George entered the shed, he felt his head giddy and his heart sick.

"Is it possible,—is it possible?" said he, kneeling down by him. "Uncle Tom, my poor, poor old friend!"

Something in the voice penetrated to the ear of the dying. He moved his head gently, smiled, and said,

108

"Jesus can make a dying-bed
Feel soft as downy pillows are."

Tears which did honor to his manly heart fell from the young man's eyes, as he bent over his poor friend.

"O, dear Uncle Tom! do wake,—do speak once more! Look up! Here's Mas'r George,—your own little Mas'r George. Don't you know me?"

"Mas'r George!" said Tom, opening his eyes, and speaking in a feeble voice; "Mas'r George!" He looked bewildered.

Slowly the idea seemed to fill his soul; and the vacant eyes became fixed and brightened, the whole face lighted up, the hard hands clasped, and tears ran down the cheeks.

"Bless the Lord! it is,—it is,—it's all I wanted! They haven't forgot me. It warms my soul; it does my old heart good! Now I shall die content! Bless the Lord, oh my soul!"

"You shan't die! you *mustn't* die, nor think of it! I've come to buy you, and take you home," said George, with impetuous vehemence.

"O, Mas'r George, ye're too late. The Lord's bought me, and is going to take me home,—and I long to go. Heaven is better than Kintuck."

"O, don't die! It'll kill me!—it'll break my heart to think what you've suffered,—and lying in this old shed, here! Poor, poor fellow!"

"Don't call me poor fellow!" said Tom, solemnly. "I *have* been poor fellow; but that's all past and gone, now. I'm right in the door, going into glory! O, Mas'r George! *Heaven has come!* I've got the victory!—the Lord Jesus has given it to me! Glory be to His name!"

George was awe-struck at the force, the vehemence, the power, with which these broken sentences were uttered. He sat gazing in silence.

Tom grasped his hand, and continued,—"Ye mustn't, now, tell Chloe, poor soul! how ye found me;—'t would be so dreful to her. Only tell her ye found me going into glory; and that I couldn't stay for no one. And tell her the Lord's stood by me everywhere and al'ays, and made everything light and easy. And oh, the poor chil'en, and the baby!—my old heart's been most broke for 'em, time and agin! Tell 'em all to follow me—follow me! Give my love to Mas'r, and dear good Missis, and everybody in the place! Ye don't know! 'Pears like I loves 'em all! I loves every creatur' everywhar!—it's nothing *but* love! O, Mas'r George! what a thing 't is to be a Christian!"

At this moment, Legree sauntered up to the door of the shed, looked in, with a dogged air of affected carelessness, and turned away.

"The old satan!" said George, in his indignation. "It's a comfort to think the devil will pay *him* for this, some of these days!"

"O, don't!—oh, ye mustn't!" said Tom, grasping his hand; "he's a poor mis'able critter! it's awful to think on 't! Oh, if he only could repent, the Lord would forgive him now; but I'm 'feared he never will!"

"I hope he won't!" said George; "I never want to see *him* in heaven!"

"Hush, Mas'r George!—it worries me! Don't feel so! He an't done me no real harm,—only opened the gate of the kingdom for me; that's all!"

At this moment, the sudden flush of strength which the joy of meeting his young master had infused into the dying man gave way. A sudden sinking fell upon him; he closed his eyes; and that mysterious and sublime change passed over his face, that told the approach of other worlds.

He began to draw his breath with long, deep inspirations; and his broad chest rose and fell, heavily. The expression of his face was that of a conqueror.

"Who,—who,—who shall separate us from the love of Christ?" he said, in a voice that contended with mortal weakness; and, with a smile, he fell asleep.

George sat fixed with solemn awe. It seemed to him that the place was holy; and, as he closed the lifeless eyes, and rose up from the dead, only one thought possessed him,—that expressed by his simple old friend,—"What a thing it is to be a Christian!"

He turned: Legree was standing, sullenly, behind him.

Something in that dying scene had checked the natural fierceness of youthful passion. The presence of the man was simply loathsome to George; and he felt only an impulse to get away from him, with as few words as possible.

Fixing his keen dark eyes on Legree, he simply said, pointing to the dead, "You have got all you ever can of him. What shall I pay you for the body? I will take it away, and bury it decently."

"I don't sell dead niggers," said Legree, doggedly. "You are welcome to bury him where and when you like."

"Boys," said George, in an authoritative tone, to two or three negroes, who were looking at the body, "help me lift him up, and carry him to my wagon; and get me a spade."

One of them ran for a spade; the other two assisted George to carry the body to the wagon.

George neither spoke to nor looked at Legree, who did not countermand his orders, but stood, whistling, with an air of forced unconcern. He sulkily followed them to where the wagon stood at the door.

George spread his cloak in the wagon, and had the body carefully disposed of in it,—moving the seat, so as to give it room. Then he turned, fixed his eyes on Legree, and said, with forced composure,

"I have not, as yet, said to you what I think of this most atrocious affair;—this is not the time and place. But, sir, this innocent blood shall have justice. I will proclaim this murder. I will go to the very first magistrate, and expose you."

"Do!" said Legree, snapping his fingers, scornfully. "I'd like to see you doing it. Where you going to get witnesses?—how you going to prove it?—Come, now!"

George saw, at once, the force of this defiance. There was not a white person on the place; and, in all southern courts, the testimony of colored blood is nothing. He felt, at that moment, as if he could have rent the heavens with his heart's indignant cry for justice; but in vain.

"After all, what a fuss, for a dead nigger!" said Legree.

The word was as a spark to a powder magazine. Prudence was never a cardinal virtue of the Kentucky boy. George turned, and, with one indignant blow, knocked Legree flat upon his face; and, as he stood over him, blazing with wrath and defiance, he would have formed no bad personification of his great namesake triumphing over the dragon.

Some men, however, are decidedly bettered by being knocked down. If a man lays them fairly flat in the dust, they seem immediately to conceive a respect for him; and Legree was one of this sort. As he rose, therefore, and brushed the dust from his clothes, he eyed the slowly-retreating wagon with some evident consideration; nor did he open his mouth till it was out of sight.

Beyond the boundaries of the plantation, George had noticed a dry, sandy knoll, shaded by a few trees: there they made the grave.

"Shall we take off the cloak, Mas'r?" said the negroes, when the grave was ready.

"No, no,—bury it with him! It's all I can give you, now, poor Tom, and you shall have it."

They laid him in; and the men shovelled away, silently. They banked it up, and laid green turf over it.

"You may go, boys," said George, slipping a quarter into the hand of each. They lingered about, however.

"If young Mas'r would please buy us—" said one.

"We'd serve him so faithful!" said the other.

"Hard times here, Mas'r!" said the first. "Do, Mas'r, buy us, please!"

"I can't!—I can't!" said George, with difficulty, motioning them off; "it's impossible!"

The poor fellows looked dejected, and walked off in silence.

"Witness, eternal God!" said George, kneeling on the grave of his poor friend; "oh, witness, that, from this hour, I will do *what one man can* to drive out this curse of slavery from my land!"

There is no monument to mark the last resting-place of our friend. He needs none! His Lord knows where he lies, and will raise him up, immortal, to appear with him when he shall appear in his glory.

Pity him not! Such a life and death is not for pity! Not in the riches of omnipotence is the chief glory of God; but in self-denying, suffering love! And blessed are the men whom he calls to fellowship with him, bearing their cross after him with patience. Of such it is written, "Blessed are they that mourn, for they shall be comforted."

Source Notes

Introduction: The Book That Started a Great War

1. Abraham Lincoln, *Selected Speeches and Writings*. New York: Vintage Books, 1992, p. 131.
2. Quoted in Joan D. Hedrick, *Harriet Beecher Stowe: A Life*. New York: Oxford University Press, 1994, p. vii.

Chapter 1: Slavery in America: 1619–1850

3. Quoted in Philip S. Foner, ed., *The Basic Writings of Thomas Jefferson*. Garden City, NY: Halcyon House, 1950, p. 24.
4. Quoted in Catherine Drinker Bowen, *Miracle at Philadelphia: The Story of the Constitutional Convention*. New York: Book-of-the-Month Club, 1986, p. 47.
5. Quoted in Foner, *The Basic Writings of Thomas Jefferson*, p. 767.
6. Quoted in Diane Ravitch, ed., *The American Reader: Words That Moved a Nation*. New York: HarperCollins, 1990, p. 100.
7. Quoted in George M. Fredrickson, ed., *William Lloyd Garrison*. Englewood Cliffs, NJ: Prentice-Hall, 1968, p. 23.
8. Quoted in James M. McPherson, *Battle Cry of Freedom: The Civil War Era*. New York: Oxford University Press, 1988, p. 82.
9. Henry David Thoreau, *Civil Disobedience and Other Essays*. New York: Dover, 1993, p. 23.
10. Quoted in Hedrick, *Harriet Beecher Stowe*, p. 207.
11. Quoted in Hedrick, *Harriet Beecher Stowe*, p. 207.

Chapter 2: The Novelist and Her Great Novel

12. Quoted in Hedrick, *Harriet Beecher Stowe*, p. 191.
13. Quoted in Hedrick, *Harriet Beecher Stowe*, p. 193.
14. Quoted in Hedrick, *Harriet Beecher Stowe*, p. 205.
15. Quoted in Josephine Donovan, Uncle Tom's Cabin: *Evil, Affliction, and Redemptive Love*. Boston: Twayne, 1991, p. xv.
16. Quoted in Hedrick, *Harriet Beecher Stowe*, p. 208.
17. Harriet Beecher Stowe, *Uncle Tom's Cabin*, ed. Elizabeth Ammons. New York: W. W. Norton, 1994, p. 8.
18. Stowe, *Uncle Tom's Cabin*, p. 69.
19. Stowe, *Uncle Tom's Cabin*, p. 48.
20. Stowe, *Uncle Tom's Cabin*, p. 294.
21. Stowe, *Uncle Tom's Cabin*, p. 293.
22. Stowe, *Uncle Tom's Cabin*, p. 296.
23. Stowe, *Uncle Tom's Cabin*, p. 298.
24. Stowe, *Uncle Tom's Cabin*, pp. 302–303.

25. Stowe, *Uncle Tom's Cabin*, p. 309.
26. Stowe, *Uncle Tom's Cabin*, p. 363.
27. Stowe, *Uncle Tom's Cabin*, p. 380.
28. Stowe, *Uncle Tom's Cabin*, p. 384.
29. Stowe, *Uncle Tom's Cabin*, p. 388.

Chapter 3: The Sources of Stowe's Novel
30. Stowe, *Uncle Tom's Cabin*, p. 388.
31. Thoreau, *Civil Disobedience and Other Essays*, pp. 2–8.
32. Stowe, *Uncle Tom's Cabin*, pp. 68–69.
33. Stowe, *Uncle Tom's Cabin*, p. 57
34. Stowe, *Uncle Tom's Cabin*, p. 199.
35. Quoted in Virginia Bernhard and Elizabeth Fox-Genovese, eds., *The Birth of American Feminism: The Seneca Falls Woman's Convention of 1848.* St. James, NY: Brandywine, 1995, pp. 85–88.
36. Ann Douglas, Introduction to *Uncle Tom's Cabin, or Life Among the Lowly,* by Harriett Beecher Stowe. New York: Penguin Books, 1981, p. 13.
37. Stowe, *Uncle Tom's Cabin*, p. 30.
38. Stowe, *Uncle Tom's Cabin*, p. 122.

Chapter 4: The War to End American Slavery
39. McPherson, *Battle Cry of Freedom*, p. 89.
40. Quoted in McPherson, *The Battle Cry of Freedom*, p. 90.
41. Quoted in Thomas F. Gossett, Uncle Tom's Cabin *and American Culture.* Dallas: Southern Methodist University Press, 1985, p. 167.
42. Quoted in William Dudley, ed., *Slavery: Opposing Viewpoints.* San Diego: Greenhaven Press, 1992, pp. 236–37.
43. Quoted in Gossett, Uncle Tom's Cabin *and American Culture,* pp. 310–11.
44. Lincoln, *Selected Speeches and Writings*, pp. 284–93.
45. Lincoln, *Selected Speeches and Writings*, p. 345.
46. Lincoln, *Selected Speeches and Writings*, p. 368.
47. Lincoln, *Selected Speeches and Writings*, p. 131.
48. Lincoln, *Selected Speeches and Writings*, p. 405.
49. Lincoln, *Selected Speeches and Writings*, p. 449.
50. Lincoln, *Selected Speeches and Writings*, p. 450.

Chapter 5: The Legacy of *Uncle Tom's Cabin*
51. Quoted in Gossett, Uncle Tom's Cabin *and American Culture,* p. 341.
52. Quoted in Gossett, Uncle Tom's Cabin *and American Culture,* p. 342.

53. Quoted in Gossett, Uncle Tom's Cabin *and American Culture*, p. 345.
54. Quoted in Gossett, Uncle Tom's Cabin *and American Culture*, p. 359.
55. Alfred Kazin, Introduction to *Uncle Tom's Cabin* by Harriet Beecher Stowe. New York: Bantam Books, 1981, p. vii.
56. Quoted in Gossett, Uncle Tom's Cabin *and American Culture*, p. 172.
57. Stowe, *Uncle Tom's Cabin*, p. 344.
58. Quoted in Gossett, Uncle Tom's Cabin *and American Culture*, p. 362.
59. Quoted in Gossett, Uncle Tom's Cabin *and American Culture*, p. 362.
60. James Baldwin, *Notes of a Native Son*. Boston: Beacon, 1984, p. 3.
61. Baldwin, *Notes of a Native Son*, p. 14.
62. Baldwin, *Notes of a Native Son*, p. 18.
63. Quoted in Gossett, Uncle Tom's Cabin *and American Culture*, p. 398.
64. Quoted in Gossett, Uncle Tom's Cabin *and American Culture*, pp. 399–400.
65. Quoted in Eric J. Sundquist, ed., *New Essays on* Uncle Tom's Cabin. New York: Cambridge University Press, 1986, p. 86.
66. Quoted in Stowe, *Uncle Tom's Cabin*, p. 502.

For Further Reading

John R. Adams, *Harriet Beecher Stowe*. Rev. ed. Boston: Twayne, 1989. This text offers an excellent introduction to Stowe's life and literary works.

Elizabeth Ammons, ed., *Critical Essays on Harriet Beecher Stowe*. Boston: G. K. Hall, 1980. This volume contains reviews and critical essays on *Uncle Tom's Cabin* and other Stowe works.

Annie Fields, ed., *Life and Letters of Harriet Beecher Stowe*. Boston: Houghton Mifflin, 1898. This volume includes selected letters written by Stowe, with commentary by the editor, from 1820 through 1896.

Stephen B. Oates, *The Approaching Fury: Voices of the Storm, 1820–1861*. New York: Harper & Row, 1970. Using first-person narration, Oates allows thirteen key figures, including Harriet Beecher Stowe, Frederick Douglass, Nat Turner, John Brown, and Abraham Lincoln, to recount the events of the decades preceding the start of the Civil War.

Charles Edward Stowe, *Life of Harriet Beecher Stowe Compiled from Her Letters and Journals*. Boston: Houghton Mifflin, 1889. This is the first biography of Stowe, written by her youngest son.

Geoffrey C. Ward, Ric Burns, and Ken Burns, *The Civil War: An Illustrated History*. New York: Knopf, 1990. This history of the Civil War, based on the award-winning documentary film, takes readers, through text, illustrations, and interviews, from the arrival of America's first slaves through the end of the Civil War.

Works Consulted

James Baldwin, *Notes of a Native Son*. Boston: Beacon, 1984. This collection of Baldwin's essays contains "Everybody's Protest Novel," his influential analysis of *Uncle Tom's Cabin*.

Virginia Bernhard and Elizabeth Fox-Genovese, eds., *The Birth of American Feminism: The Seneca Falls Woman's Convention of 1848*. St. James, NY: Brandywine, 1995. This volume includes documents relating to the Seneca Falls women's rights convention of 1848.

Catherine Drinker Bowen, *Miracle at Philadelphia: The Story of the Constitutional Convention*. New York: Book-of-the-Month Club, 1986. This detailed history of the Philadelphia Convention of 1787 includes discussions of how the framers of the U.S. Constitution dealt with the issue of slavery.

Ann Douglas, Introduction to *Uncle Tom's Cabin, or Life Among the Lowly* by Harriett Beecher Stowe. New York: Penguin Books, 1981. This introduction to *Uncle Tom's Cabin* discusses Stowe's feminist leanings.

Josephine Dovovan, Uncle Tom's Cabin: *Evil, Affliction, and Redemptive Love*. Boston: Twayne, 1991. This text offers a detailed analysis of *Uncle Tom's Cabin*, including a discussion of its sources and its critical reception.

William Dudley, ed., *Slavery: Opposing Viewpoints*. San Diego: Greenhaven Press, 1992. This collection of documents on slavery provides the arguments of both the institution's defenders and those dedicated to its abolition.

Philip S. Foner, ed., *The Basic Writings of Thomas Jefferson*. Garden City, NY. Halcyon House, 1950. This collection of Jefferson's writings contains both the first and final drafts of the Declaration of Independence.

George M. Fredrickson, ed., *William Lloyd Garrison*. Englewood Cliffs, NJ: Prentice-Hall, 1968. This anthology offers a collection of some of Garrison's most important writings, including several pieces from the *Liberator*.

Thomas F. Gossett, Uncle Tom's Cabin *and American Culture*. Dallas: Southern Methodist University Press, 1985. This study of *Uncle Tom's Cabin* traces the novel's place in American history from its creation through the 1980s.

Joan D. Hedrick, *Harriet Beecher Stowe: A Life*. New York: Oxford University Press, 1994. This award-winning biography of Stowe captures her life and the spirit of the turbulent times in which she lived.

Alfred Kazin, Introduction to *Uncle Tom's Cabin,* by Harriett Beecher Stowe. New York: Bantam Books, 1981. This introduction to *Uncle Tom's Cabin* traces the novel's reception in the nineteenth century and by readers of today.

Abraham Lincoln, *Selected Speeches and Writings.* New York: Vintage Books, 1992. This single-volume collection contains Lincoln's most important speeches and writings.

James M. McPherson, *Battle Cry of Freedom: The Civil War Era.* New York: Oxford University Press, 1988. McPherson's text details the period of American history from the 1850s through the Civil War.

Diane Ravitch, ed., *The American Reader: Words That Moved a Nation.* New York: HarperCollins, 1990. This anthology collects key American texts, including several associated with the abolitionist movement and the Civil War.

Harriet Beecher Stowe, *Uncle Tom's Cabin.* Ed. Elizabeth Ammons. New York: W. W. Norton, 1994. This edition of the novel is accompanied by background materials, reviews, and contemporary critical articles, including Jane Tompkins's feminist analysis of *Uncle Tom's Cabin.*

Eric J. Sundquist, ed., *New Essays on* Uncle Tom's Cabin. New York: Cambridge University Press, 1986. This collection of essays contains feminist readings of *Uncle Tom's Cabin* by Jean Fagan Yellin and Elizabeth Ammons.

Henry David Thoreau, *Civil Disobedience and Other Essays.* New York: Dover, 1993. This collection of Thoreau's essays contains "Civil Disobedience," "Slavery in Massachusetts," and "A Plea for Captain John Brown."

Index

Picture Credits

About the Author

James Tackach is the author of *Brown v. Board of Education*, *The Trial of John Brown*, *The Emancipation Proclamation*, and young adult biographies of Roy Campanella, Henry Aaron, and James Baldwin. He has also authored *Historic Homes of America*, *Great American Hotels*, and *Fields of Summer: America's Great Ballparks and the Players Who Triumphed in Them*. His articles have appeared in the *New York Times*, *Providence Journal*, *America's Civil War*, and a variety of academic publications. Dr. Tackach teaches in the English Department at Roger Williams University, Bristol, Rhode Island, and lives in Narragansett, Rhode Island.